MAY 2012

THE MAGIC MAKER

THE MAGIC MAKER

*A Portrait of John Langstaff,
Creator of the Christmas Revels*

SUSAN COOPER

CANDLEWICK PRESS

First edition 2011

Library of Congress Cataloging-in-Publication Data
Cooper, Susan, date.
The magic maker : a portrait of John Langstaff, creator of the Christmas Revels / Susan Cooper. — 1st ed.
p.   cm.
ISBN 978-0-7636-5040-7
1. Langstaff, John M.   2. Baritones (Singers) — United States — Biography.
3. Theatrical producers and directors — United States — Biography.
4. Revels, Inc.   I. Title.
ML420.L2383C66 2011
780.92 — dc22[B]   2010053682

11 12 13 14 15 16 RRC 10 9 8 7 6 5 4 3 2 1

Printed in Crawfordsville, IN, U.S.A.

This book was typeset in Minion.

Candlewick Press
99 Dover Street
Somerville, Massachusetts 02144

visit us at www.candlewick.com

for Tro

and for Carol, John, Gary,
Deborah, and Caitlin

FOREWORD

*A*ny Christmastime, at Harvard University's Sanders Theatre, in Cambridge, Massachusetts. The snow is deep outside. Into the cavernous, echoing lobby stream hundreds of families, all the generations mixed, coat-wrapped and scarf-wound, their breath clouding in the cold air. Christmas is in their heads, and this is a peak of it: their anticipated celebration, familiar as Mass to a Catholic or pantomime to an English child. The happy thunderous babel of voices washes over you like a sea.

"The dragon with the big claws," says a very small boy insistently, "will the dragon be there, like last year?"

"Betty!" cries one harried mother to another, barely visible through the bobbing heads of her tribe. "I never see you except at the Revels!"

"Wouldn't be Christmas without it."

"Daddy's going to sing the carols," says a small confident girl.

"You sing, I'll listen," says her lugubrious father through his overcoat collar.

The lights go down, the voices hush, and the families are deep suddenly in reawakened echoes of winter festivals from two thousand years past: pagan and Christian, Celtic and Nordic, Anglo-Saxon and Hebrew, and a dozen other cultures. A clear solo voice sings the lilting Hebridean "Christ Child's Lullaby"; eerily horned dancers stalk through a fertility dance as old as Stonehenge; in a bright swirl of medieval costume, a procession of musicians and chorus sings its way through the house to the stage. The dragon duly cavorts; beribboned Morris men leap and dance; a troupe of players brings brave Sir Gawain to challenge the Green Knight. The audience roars, laughs, sings, and at last finds itself winding in an immense singing, dancing line through the crowded lobby, led by a smiling, dark-haired man whose voice rises strong over the rest:

> *Dance, then, wherever you may be,*
> *I am the Lord of the Dance, said he . . .*

And the lugubrious father is singing and dancing there too in the throng, overcoat flapping wide, a look of bemused delight on his face.

We stand, John Meredith Langstaff and I, in the dim-lit theater, among the empty seats, discussing a forthcoming spring production of the Revels. He waves at the air: "I want a great forty-foot mast to go up, in Act One, right here. Men hoisting it, singing sea chanteys the way they were meant to be sung."

"That's lovely, but it's crazy. We'll hit that chandelier."

"There's some marvelous material — windlass chanteys, chanteys for hoisting sail —"

"Too dangerous. And what about the sight lines?"

He says craftily, "We could have the mast sway, in that storm at the end of your seal story. Wouldn't that be great?"

"It won't work, Jack. We might brain half the audience. It'll be too heavy. Too complicated. Too —"

Three months later, a thousand people cheer as a tall shining mast rises dramatically in the middle of Sanders Theatre, bringing timeworn sea chanteys vividly alive. When the artistic director of the Revels has dreams, they tend to come true. . . .

In the thirty years since I wrote those words in *The Horn Book Magazine*, John Langstaff's Revels has spread across the United States: its Christmas — and spring or summer — productions are a seasonal landmark not only in Cambridge but in Hanover, New Hampshire, in New York City, in Washington, D.C., in Oakland and Santa Barbara, California, in Houston, Texas, in Tacoma, Washington, in Portland, Oregon, and in Boulder, Colorado. It has spawned similar celebrations in many smaller towns, the range of outreach work is enormous, and the scope of the whole network continues to evolve under its new leaders. An idea has become an institution. The major beacons in all the arts depend not only on artists, performing or creative, but on Makers: charismatic visionaries like Joseph Papp, Jacques d'Amboise, Tyrone Guthrie, Martha Graham — and John Langstaff.

As you may know from experience, it's hard to define the Revels. It is not commercial theater; it isn't folksy; it isn't a concert; it is neither religious nor pagan — yet it combines certain strong elements from all these into a peculiar form of theatrical magic. The National Endowment for the Arts, giving Revels a grant in its early days, called it "a new and different form of musical theater." Using

3

a core of professionals and a chorus of amateur singers, Langstaff contrived to weave song, dance, and drama into a celebration of the winter solstice. He hit a nerve, providing an answer to that submerged yearning for ritual, and for the marking of ancient landmarks in human life, which lies very deep in all of us and which very little in the American Way can satisfy. (In Britain, that same yearning is probably the reason why the monarchy survives.) Telling signs of emotion have always appeared in letters from the fiercely possessive audiences who buy out every Revels production in every city: "I can't remember the last time I felt such a personal involvement in a performance," ran one typical example. "I left with an incredible glow of joy."

I am a writer, mostly of books published for children, though overall I'm more of a GP than a specialist. I joined the Revels family in 1975, after being recruited by Jack (nobody ever called him "John" for more than five minutes) backstage at the previous year's Christmas production. For the next twenty years I wrote verse, short plays, stories, lyrics, program notes, record notes, and any other words Jack felt he needed. We became working partners, linked by respect, understanding, and the pleasure of the job we were doing; we grew to know most of each other's strengths, failings, and foibles, and when he died in 2005 I lost one of my three closest friends.

A year or so before that, after a series of tentative references to "a project I'd like to talk to you about," he had announced that he wanted to write a book that he thought would be called *The Choirboy.* "Starting with that extraordinary childhood of mine, going away to choir school for years at the age of seven. I've been thinking about it a lot — so much that happened later must have been sparked back then. . . . Will you help me?"

"Of course," I said.

But time ran out on us. So I'm doing it for him, using our notes, his papers, my own files and tapes, and some invaluable recordings made by the Revels' Music Director, George Emlen, and its Marketing Director, Alan Casso. I owe particular gratitude not only to George and Alan but to Gayle Rich, to Nancy, Carol, Deborah, and David Langstaff, to Paddy Swanson, Brian Holmes, Sue Ladr, Roger Ide, David Coffin, Jerry Epstein, Jay O'Callahan, and many others. This is not a full Langstaff biography, nor a history of the thriving, complex organization that Revels, Inc., has become today, but it shows, I hope, how Jack Langstaff's Revels began.

Here is a portrait of one of the Makers, and — now and again — a personal record of a working friendship.

CHAPTER ONE

THE CHOIRBOY

On the morning of April 6, 1918, the film star Douglas Fairbanks (senior) flashed his gleaming teeth on the steps of the New York Stock Exchange and launched a Liberty Loan drive "to support our brave soldiers." It had taken the United States three years to join in the Great War that had been devastating Europe since 1914, but now public opinion supported President Wilson so enthusiastically that the drive would raise more than $4 billion ($60 billion in modern terms) within a month.

The peril of war is a great promoter of matrimony. In another part of New York that day, one of those brave American soldiers was getting married. Captain Bridgewater Meredith Langstaff of the 77th Infantry Division was thirty-three, tall, dark, and dashing, and his bride, Esther Knox Boardman, was vivacious, very pretty, and just nineteen years old. It was an ironic pre-echo: though this was supposed to be "the war to end all wars," twenty-five years later their first son would be propelled into marriage with an eighteen-year-old by another world war.

After the Armistice of 1918, the Langstaffs set up house in Brooklyn Heights: first in Columbia Heights, then in a three-story brownstone at 39 Garden Place. Meredith, a lawyer who eventually specialized in public utility cases, had been born in Brooklyn. He came from a long line of Langstaffs with roots in the north of England and a genetic tendency to independence of spirit. The first American Langstaff, Henry, had come to New Hampshire in 1605, and his descendants moved initially to New Jersey (to escape the Puritans spreading north from Massachusetts) and later, being loyal to the Crown, to Canada (to escape the Revolution). But Meredith's father, John, a doctor, moved back in the nineteenth century from Canada to practice in New York, and he sent his sons to Harvard.

Meredith was class of 1908, along with the cardiologist Paul Dudley White and the historian Samuel Eliot Morison, and went afterward to Columbia Law School. Eventually he became part of a New York partnership called Donovan, Leisure, Newton, Lumbard, and Irvine. The firm had been founded by another Columbia Law graduate, William "Wild Bill" Donovan, who also founded the OSS, precursor of the CIA. ("My father had an amazing range of friends," said Jack Langstaff once, "including a famous spy.")

Pretty Esther Langstaff may have been fourteen years younger than her husband, but she was a remarkable girl, from a cultivated and intensely musical family. Her mother had a very high coloratura soprano voice and had given concerts in Paris, and Esther's brother Arthur inherited the vocal talent and became a notable Wagnerian tenor. Esther sang too, but was usually to be found at the piano; she was an instinctive pianist, of the kind who can play almost anything at sight, or by ear. Perhaps she never regretted choosing marriage over a formal musical training; perhaps there was no element of frustrated ambition in the phenomenal energy with which, later, she propelled her firstborn son into a career as a singer. At all events she was to become, among many other things, an accomplished example of what is now called the Theater Mom.

Meredith and Esther's first child died, stillborn perhaps, in 1919. There's no knowing whether young Esther deliberately decided that her second should be a Christmas baby, but he certainly was. Family legend has it that she ran up and down the stairs and moved heavy furniture around to encourage labor to begin, and sure enough, John Meredith Langstaff was born on Christmas Eve, December 24, 1920. When he was two, the little family moved to the house at 39 Garden Place and rapidly put down roots; before long Meredith had founded the Garden Place Association, and he remained its president for the next fifty-four years.

Number 39 was full of music. There was a constant stream of visiting musicians, not one grand piano but two, and a rousing carol party every Christmas, on the Sunday before Christmas Day. Jack's father too sang; he had what Jack later described as "a nice lyric tenor voice," and he had sung in the glee club at Harvard. He had also grown up in a home where (as he once told a newspaper with the splendid name of *The Brooklyn Heights Press and Cobble Hill News*) his mother held a salon every Wednesday evening "and all the stars of the opera companies would gather to sing and give recitals." And it was music that had introduced him to Esther. Posted to Camp Upton, Long Island, he had organized a Christmas party for lonely soldiers, and had found himself singing to the piano accompaniment of "a beautiful and talented young lady who was a neighbor of our host for the evening." They were married four months later.

9

It's quite likely that Jack Langstaff began to sing before he could walk or even talk. He probably heard his family's first carol party from the womb, since it was held five days before he was born. (After Meredith died, at ninety-seven, his sons found four books detailing all the Christmas party carols — dating from 1920.) By the time he was five years old he had two brothers, Kennedy and David; their one sister, Esther, later known as Terry, was born in 1929, when her mother was thirty, and was the last of the children. There are some fairy-tale photographs of the beautiful children and their beautiful young mother.

The carol parties were always a peak of the family's year, with the smell of hot wassail — spiced wine, rather than the traditional medieval English spiced ale, cider, or mead — drifting up through the house from the kitchen. So many friends came that the boys would be dispatched beforehand on frequent trips to the Episcopal church around the corner, tugging their little wooden wagons, to bring back loads of borrowed folding chairs. Jack said, fifty years later, remembering:

> *The house would be crowded with people, a candlelit house, with my mother at one piano and someone else at the other, and my father and his friends would sing carols — he must have collected three or four hundred carols from all over the world. Everyone sang — we did "The Twelve Days of Christmas" as a family, with everyone acting out parts — we did canons and rounds, eventually we even did Bach chorales. There were people of all sorts of religions there; it didn't matter, they all sang.*

Meredith always sang his own solo carol, "King Herod and the Cock," with Esther at the piano; he was still singing it at ninety-six, not long before he died, though by then a little shaky on the order of the verses. While the boys were young they took turns singing the Page to their father's Good King Wenceslas; all three of them had clear, true soprano voices in childhood. Jack's particular solo was the haunting "I Wonder As I Wander"; he had learned it from its composer, John Jacob Niles, who briefly came, dulcimer and lute in hand, as one of the musical visitors to this very musical house.

And it was Jack's voice, and its care and training, that became Esther's mission.

"We all sang music every night, with her at the piano," he said. "I don't know why she concentrated on me. She always believed in it, somehow. As far back as I can remember, I sang, she accompanied me. She insisted on the right intonation — it couldn't be even a little bit off. And she was very hot on diction, whether it was clean enough. Then when I was seven, she decided I should sing in a choir, so she took me to the choirmaster at the church two blocks away."

Jack was not only very young but very thin, and the choirmaster at Brooklyn Heights' Grace Church told Esther that she should bring him back when he had grown up a little. Esther paid this absolutely no attention. Instead she carried Jack off to another Grace Church, the beautiful, lofty neo-Gothic Episcopal church on the corner of Broadway and 10th Street in Manhattan; her *entrée* there was perhaps the fact that her brother-in-law had at some point been its assistant minister. Ernest Mitchell, the choirmaster at this Grace Church, had not only a celebrated choir but a choir school; it was the oldest in New York City, founded in 1894 for 16 boy sopranos (and surviving today as Grace Church School, for 400 boys and girls up to 8th grade).

So seven-year-old Jack faced Mr. Mitchell and sang Stainer's "God So Loved the World" with his mother at the piano, and

Mitchell offered him a place at the choir school and helped to mold his life forever.

It was a boarding school, next door to the church, and the boys were allowed to see their parents only on Sundays, for three hours. The change in small Jack's world must have been drastic; up to this point he had been spending half days at the progressive Woodward School ("Maybe Father could afford it then"), which had just been founded in Brooklyn. Now, off he went to the Grace Church Choir School, and stayed there for five years. He was away from home during the summers too, with a singing scholarship at a music camp for boys. Music enveloped his life completely.

He later claimed he was never homesick.

I wasn't lonely, missing my parents — well, probably at first, but they kept you so busy. It was all rehearsals, going, going, going. Mitchell was a wonderful teacher. The way he trained our voices . . . it wasn't the usual hootie-flootie sound that you hear in cathedrals in England, it had a ring to it. And he was an outstanding organist, a great technician, with all the repertoire including the then far-out music of Charles Tournamine, who'd been a pupil of César Franck. All the young organists about town used to turn up at our Evensong services, to hear Mitchell and his boy choir.

Within two years, Jack was the choir's soloist. Esther was still a busy background influence during his years at the choir school. She took him to sing for the celebrated organist Norman Coke-Jephcott at the Cathedral of St. John the Divine and for David Mackay at St. Bartholomew's Church, and both men later hired him to sing soprano solos with their adult choirs. Since the Grace Church choirboys were paid for their singing at weddings and funerals, before he was ten years old Jack was making a welcome contribution to his family's income — the Great Depression having had its effect on the Langstaffs just as on every other American household.

Eventually Jack had a gig at CBS Radio as well. "My mother would pick me up at five AM and we'd be at CBS to perform by seven, along with all kinds of soloists and some awful poetry. . . . They'd pay me twenty dollars, or even fifty, and that was a lot then." His repertoire included all the classic pieces then sung by boy sopranos, like "O for the Wings of a Dove," but it also went way beyond. David Blair McCloskey, the singer-teacher who was John Fitzgerald Kennedy's voice coach in his 1960 campaign, once reminisced about singing the baritone part in a performance of the Brahms *Requiem* in which young Jack Langstaff sang soprano.

Two years after Jack became a chorister, his brother Kennedy joined him. Since Ken had a tendency to sleepwalk, Jack was charged with looking after him. "He'd go toward the window, and I'd go and put a chair in his way." Ken too had a beautiful voice, but he had not been given his brother's sense that his voice was his identity. He was much less restrained than Jack in expressing his longing to be back at 39 Garden Place. Esther Langstaff kept every letter that her children ever wrote her, and after they had grown up she chose the letters she felt should be preserved, typed them all out, and had them compiled in seven leather-bound books. The two elder boys' letters from choir school show a telling contrast.

Here is Jack at twelve, writing home on Mother's Day 1933.

Dear Mother,

I love you so much that it is very hard to write because it would take up so much room.

I am very grateful to you, and I know I would not be

making so much money and things like that if it were not for you teaching me how to sing, and I would never sing if it weren't for you. And I hope our family will never be seperated [sic] for a very long time.

With love, Jack

P.S. "I love you"

And here is Ken at the same age, two years later, writing a letter headed *VERY PRIVATE VERY.*

Dear Mother and Daddy,

I do not want to upset you, but what I am about to tell you is not recent. I have been hinting a little to Daddy. I would like to be a <u>Day Boy</u>*.*

The reasons why are: I am and was very, very homesick for you and Daddy. I wouldn't get into half as much trouble in school. I could help you a lot (though I am not so good at that). I would like it better running errands and sitting with you at the nighttime. I love the choir and I like Mr. Mitchell very much. And I like the school pretty well. . . . I don't get and neither does Jack get time enough to get help on our work. And you or Daddy could help us. The main point is, if you only <u>knew how</u> homesick <u>we</u> are for you. We don't get enough time to see you. The expenses are about the same because the laundry is $30 and our food and carfare would be about that much and if not we could earn from funeral singing. PLEASE don't let it upset you. But I would like to be a <u>Day Boy</u>*. Just write or tell me <u>yes</u> or <u>no</u> at the bottom. Please don't get <u>Mad</u>.*

With much love,

Kennedy Langstaff

This heartrending appeal had no effect, though it does presage the warm heart and diplomatic skills of the adult Ken Langstaff. Both boys remained boarders. Sometimes they would be allowed to go home for their three-hour release on Sundays; sometimes their parents would come to visit them at the school. "Ken and I would take them out to Longchamps," Jack said, referring to an upscale New York restaurant chain. "We'd have a malted, and they'd have a martini."

Jack's voice was so phenomenal that he was soon the pride of the Grace Church boys' choir; Ernest Mitchell later said he had never had a better chorister. But Mitchell had to fight to keep him. The shy, angelic choirboy had a powerful sense of mischief, and he was always in trouble. He passed notes during the sermon, forgetting that the organist could see him, and once he let marbles bounce out of his pocket down the chancel steps during the quietest part of a funeral. He was fascinated by the organ pipes, which were in separate rooms forbidden to the boys. "I'd take a friend and go up there to explore, and it was OK unless Mitchell came to practice. If he noticed we were up there he'd put on the organ's thirty-two-foot bombarde — I swear you could hear it two blocks away. . . ."

He formed a Robin Hood Band of seven or eight boys. "I was Robin Hood, and Ken was Friar Tuck because he was kind of chubby. There was Little John, Will Scarlet, all of them. . . . We made bows and arrows, and when we were taken to Central Park we'd climb up on those rocks there, rescuing fair ladies, doing good deeds."

Perhaps influenced by the nature of its home base, the band said prayers at its meetings. Here's one of them:

O Lord, help this Band to do Thy will, and to help
those who are in need. Guide our acts with wisdom
and kindness through Jesus Christ our lord. Amen.

There was also a list of rules, showing another influence: Meredith Langstaff was a scout leader for years and eventually became head of the Boy Scouts of America in the New York area. His sons never became scouts, but clearly absorbed the same upright principles.

SOME RULES FOR THE RHB
1. Reverence to God (at all times).
2. Never in any way harm a woman or child.
3. Be loyal to the Band.
4. Always obey.
5. Obey all the rules of the Boy Scouts of America.
6. Stand by and fight to the finish.

There being nothing in these rules about food, Jack was also very fond of organizing midnight feasts. "The big things I loved were green olives — we could get them at a grocery across the street — and chocolate cake. So we'd hide these, and then we'd have feasts, at night. About two thirty or three in the morning, we'd go down the corridor very quietly and sit and eat."

And sometimes they were caught. "The headmaster was a bastard — he'd sit up at night waiting, and then he'd make you stand there in your pajamas for two hours and switch you if you moved."

This didn't deter Robin Hood from a far more perilous night-time activity: leading the whole band out of the dormitory window and along the roof. They would inch their way along the ridge of the church roof to the steeple, where Jack had found the little door through which workmen got into the bell tower. In they would go, up and up, past the bells — which, as all good Dorothy Sayers fans know, can be lethal if they start to ring while you're in there with them. "We knew we had to get out by a certain time; it was exciting. And we'd crawl back along the roof. If you looked down, there was Broadway, way below. I must have been crazy. But nobody ever looked up and saw this little line of kids in their pajamas."

He was less fortunate after he took one of his band down to the crypt, where he'd discovered that the blower room for the church's heating system had a dirt floor. They were pirates this time; they had various piratical things in a box on which they'd signed their names in blood, and they buried it ceremonially under the floor. Unfortunately they kicked so much dust up into the blowers that the church began to grow unaccountably dirty. When Authority investigated the blower room, it found the signs of digging, and unearthed the box.

"And of course," said Jack, "there were our names on the top."

Authority was not pleased, and no doubt had the headmaster on its side. But not the choirmaster. "Four times the vestry said to Mitchell, 'You have to get rid of this boy.' But he didn't."

And Jack loved the singing more than the mischief. He sang "I Know That My Redeemer Liveth"; he sang "Hear Ye, Israel" and other Mendelssohn staples. "And we sang a lot of new stuff . . . Stainer, most of it awful . . . and I *think* we did the first American performance of the Vaughan Williams Mass. That kind of music really made an impression on me. I was convinced that I wanted to go on just singing oratorio. And besides that, I was with one of the most spiritual men I ever met in my life."

Walter Russell Bowie was the rector of Grace Episcopal Church; he was a liberal-minded Southerner who became a friend of Franklin Delano Roosevelt at Harvard, and he was in his forties when Jack was at the choir school.

"I thought the world of him, " Jack said. "His son Rusty and I used to get into a lot of trouble together. He had two daughters as well — when I was nine or ten I was madly in love with Elizabeth, aged eighteen. Dr. Bowie had a big influence on me. He used to pray specially for us before we sang, and it really made me feel a connection with God, with a presence, a very powerful thing. I really think I was singing to that, not to the congregation, and if I didn't sing well I could be really down."

He wrote an endearing essay about this when he was fourteen entitled "A Nervous Soloist."

The minister is mumbling the last prayer before I have to sing.

Many thoughts rush through my mind: "I must not flat, I must sing it joyously and skippingly, I must not be afraid."

My hands get wet and cold and my stomach feels very funny and uneasy and I wish I were home in my warm bed.

I try not to let anyone see how nervous I am and I pray that God will help me and carry me through it.

Of all the solos to be singing! Bach's "My Heart Ever Faithful," it is a fine solo but my hart [sic] is anything but faithful. My mouth is getting dry and I get a sort of lost and sissy feeling and a little faint.

I must not bite my fingernails.

Oh! If I could only have a nice long drink of pineapple juice to oil up the larynx.

The prayer is coming to an end and we sing the "Amen," I look up. There's Little John smiling at me, I guess he knows how I feel; and Scarlet over there winks at me.

The prayer ended; I get up and clear my throat and nod to Erny. He nods back and gives me a reassuring glance and starts the introduction. Only two measures to go. I must relax!! but it seems to be impossible.

I sing my first note and I regain confidence and sing

through it all right, forgetting all about the congregation and enter into the spirit of the music.

But when it is finished I want to sing it all over again.

"Erny" is of course Ernest Mitchell. He, Dr. Bowie, and the Anglican liturgy of the Episcopal Church all fostered in young Jack not only a sense of the mystical but a great taste for the theatrical side of ritual. "Easter Day was wonderful. We'd go from the school to the big room before the church — I'd lead the choristers, two by two, and we'd make a circle, just as we do backstage today before a Revels performance. Dr. Bowie would give a final prayer just for us, and then you'd hear the organ strike up, and the big doors would open and in we'd go, singing 'Welcome, Happy Morning.' Mitchell would bring in the brass, I loved that — the big organ would be going, and another one in another part of the church — it was very exciting."

Soon he was performing not only in churches and on the radio, but onstage. It began with ambitious productions of Gilbert and Sullivan operettas at the Choate School, in Wallingford, Connecticut. "The headmaster there was nuts about Gilbert and Sullivan. He put money into it — the costumes all came from Eaves, the best costumier in New York, and a wig man came up. . . . I was asked to come as a boy soprano to sing roles like Yum-Yum in *The Mikado* and Josephine in *H.M.S. Pinafore*. And then they offered me a full scholarship, and God knows my father wanted me to get a good education."

But Jack refused to leave New York. He was still singing lead soprano for Ernest Mitchell and knew Mitchell would hate to lose him, and he felt his family had always raised him with a strong sense of group loyalty. So although they now begged him to move to Choate, he wouldn't.

"There were all kinds of meetings, but I would not be swayed. So perhaps my mother said to them, 'Well, you know we have another boy, Kennedy . . .' So Ken went, and he sang Josephine — which is really high, my God — and got a scholarship and did very well."

In the summers of the depressed 1930s, all three Langstaff boys went on singing, at a little camp at the foot of Mount Washington in Bretton Woods, New Hampshire. Jack remembered vaguely that when he was really small, the family had rented a villa in the Catskills for the summer, and that when he was seven, he had been sent to Camp Wulamat, on Lake Winnipesaukee in New Hampshire, where proper little boys then wore uniforms. Now that the family fortunes were declining, he found himself at a camp designed for scholarship boys to sing to the wealthy. It turned into a remarkably useful part of his education.

Camp Duncan had its beginnings in 1910 when a summer visitor to the Mount Washington Hotel, one George Duncan, organized the Bretton Woods Boy Singers to sing in the Joseph Stickney Chapel of the Transfiguration. Stickney was the bold New Hampshire industrialist who in 1881 had bought ten thousand acres around Mount Washington, eventually building the huge Italianate hotel to attract prosperous summer visitors from Boston, New York, and beyond. He died a year after it opened, in 1903, and in his memory his young widow, Carolyn, put up a handsome gray granite chapel with magnificent Tiffany windows. Today it's a summer chapel of the Diocese of New Hampshire, with services on July and August Saturdays and a lot of weddings. And the spectacular Mount Washington Hotel, after some hard times, is a well-developed resort. (In July 1944 it was the site of the Allied powers' Bretton Woods Conference, out of which came, among other things, the International Monetary Fund (IMF) and the General Agreement on Tariffs and Trade (GATT).)

By the time Jack went to Camp Duncan in 1930, the young

widow Carolyn Stickney had reached her sixties. She had not only married again — this time acquiring a title by marrying a Frenchman named Prince Aymon de Faucigny-Lucinge — but been widowed again. She is said to have owned hotels in Paris and Switzerland as well as the Mount Washington, but every summer she came back to Bretton Woods, where the choristers knew her simply as The Princess. It was her money that gave them their free summer.

The boys' choir at Bretton Woods was now well established as "a scholarship group of outstanding boy singers from the New England area, chosen to sing on Sundays during services at the Chapel of the Transfiguration, under the training and direction of Frank Hancock." Hancock, an accomplished organist, had been hired for the job when he was twenty-two and still a graduate student at Harvard. Since 1917 he had also been music master at a school in Brooklyn, Poly Prep Country Day School, so he was a friend of the Langstaff family and a regular at the Christmas carol parties. For the New Hampshire summers he brought boys from choirs as far away as Washington, D.C. and Chicago, about fifteen of the best young singers he could find.

Hancock was known to the boys as "Uncle Frank." Their life at camp included a variety of classic outdoor activities. "I was Tarzan for a while," said Jack. "We had an Elephants' Graveyard in the woods, those kind of things. And we made rafts — cold as hell that river was." But music was the framework of their days.

"We rehearsed every day to sing at the chapel on Sundays, all of us in our little cassocks, and our white collars. Frank Hancock played the organ. We sang things like Gounod's 'Sanctus'— he trained us very well."

Every day too they rehearsed secular music, of a kind not likely to be heard in choir schools. For the summer state of New Hampshire, they were a kind of mini version of the Vienna Boys'

Choir, giving about thirty concerts in the fashionable hotels of the White Mountains. For those of them who would end up as professional singers, it was a gentle introduction to touring.

"We had to wear black knickers, white shirts, and great big black bow ties," Jack said. "And black patent leather shoes. We drove around to the concerts in a ratty old bus—Frank had hired a tenor straight from Juilliard to sing and be his assistant, and the tenor drove the bus. Some of the stuff we sang was awful—Victor Herbert, 'The Last Rose of Summer,' 'The Bells of St. Mary's.' The three Langstaff boys sang 'Three Little Maids from School,' wearing these *hats* . . . And Ken once sang ''O Promise Me'—it was a riot. But they loved it."

At thirteen, he said in a letter home:

Dear Mother and Daddy,

Thanks very much for the funny papers you sent and thanks for sending Iolanthe. *Ken already knows the Hansel and Gretel duet. We gave a concert at the Mount Washington last night and the Princess gave us another dinner and $2.50 each making $5 for Ken and I.*

Will you please give us permission in your next letter to buy maple sugar and syrup for this winter with the $5.

How is my solo medal? I hope it is not lost.

"I love you."

Jack

The money was an important part of the Bretton Woods summers. "All these wealthy people would come to the hotel concerts, and we'd all take turns passing the hat. Uncle Frank's black hat, it was. All of us except me, that is—I just couldn't bring myself to do it, going around asking for money. But at the end of the summer he'd dole it out, all these coins, dividing it according to what solos we'd had. I'd go home with maybe sixty dollars, and in the thirties that was a lot of money."

Like many performers, he was still shy, in spite of all those solos. To the end of his days, Jack Langstaff could command any audience anywhere with his professional persona, but would flinch from exposure as an unprotected private civilian. At Bretton Woods it wasn't only the prospect of passing a hat that made him recoil. "My parents borrowed a car once in a while and came up to see us — my father never drove a car but my mother loved to drive. And I'd go and hide in the woods when they arrived, because I was so shy at having them around. . . . I was incredibly shy. I could get up and sing at concerts because I felt that wasn't me, but when people came to talk to me afterward I'd just look at the floor."

The "solo medal" mentioned in his letter was a gold medal awarded him for the years he was the principal soloist in the Grace Church boys' choir. By the summer of 1935, when he was fourteen, although he had left the school, his voice had not yet broken, and he was still going back to sing solos as a paid outsider. This was the point at which he refused to go to Choate, giving up a scholarship rather than stop singing for Ernest Mitchell while he was still a soprano. Instead he went on half scholarship for some months to Poly Prep, where Frank Hancock was music master, and again went up to Hancock's Bretton Woods choir with his brothers for the summer.

Mitchell sent him a letter while he was there. This gave Jack great pleasure, but when he next wrote to his parents it was only to ask for the funny papers and a boomerang, and to report that "in one of the songs we are doing for our concert I take a high B obligato above the chorus and I can take it easy as anything." It was Ken, now twelve, who forwarded them the Mitchell letter.

> *Dear Jack,*
>
> *I enclose check for funerals. Thank you for your very nice letter in June.*
>
> *And now let me thank you for your perfectly splendid work as a choirboy and soloist at Grace Church. I have had a lot of good choirboys but never had a better one than you. In fact, I think you <u>head</u> the list! My heartfelt thanks to you, Jack, for your magnificent work in Grace Church Choir.*
>
> *Best wishes for a pleasant summer.*
>
> *And do not work your voice too long! Better save it for future years.*
>
> *Sincerely yours,*
>
> *Ernest Mitchell*

The check was for $19. Ken wrote, "Jack and I thought it best to give the money to Uncle Frank to settle our accounts. But in your next letter please tell us what to do with it. We promise not to spend it."

When that summer was over, Jack didn't go back to Poly Prep, which he said he had hated from the moment when he turned up wearing shorts and found every other boy in long pants. Instead he found himself finishing the year at the Woodward School, where once he had been in kindergarten (and where Arlo Guthrie would go into sixth grade, thirty years later). They probably let him in, he said, because his mother was teaching music there at the time.

"Mother said to me, 'I've met your teacher and you're going to like her. She loves Robin Hood.'"

The teacher was a young woman named Carol Preston. She

told Jack later that he had been so shy when they first met that when all the children were told to put their galoshes in the closet, he went into the closet and stayed there. She had to go and pull him out. The rescue was a lovely metaphor for the effect she was to have on the rest of his life; he had met another mentor. The choir-boy was about to acquire another of the talents that would lead him to the making of the Revels.

Chapter Two

"The Morris Dances
are swell"

*M*eredith Langstaff had a lively, inquiring mind and the instincts of a collector; as a result he accumulated an extensive library during his long life. When he died, he bequeathed it to the Houghton Library at Harvard, to which he had already given his collection of Andrew Lang manuscripts and letters. His fascination with Lang, the prolific mythologist and author known most widely for his collections of fairy tales (*The Blue Fairy Book, The Red Fairy Book,* and so on through the rainbow), was part of an overall interest in folktale and folk song. Both Meredith and Esther admired Cecil Sharp, the legendary English musicologist who had rescued his native folk dance and folk song from extinction, and Sharp's folk song collections were not only in the library but often on the piano. There was more than oratorio and opera in Jack Langstaff's family background.

Cecil Sharp, born in 1859, had studied law at Cambridge, but then emigrated to Australia and switched to his true love, music.

He came back to England at thirty-three as an accomplished music teacher, and is said to have had one of those life-changing moments on Boxing Day 1899, when he saw the Morris men dance in the village of Headington, Oxfordshire. Another one came four years later when he overheard his gardener singing the folk song "The Seeds of Love." Realizing that all the traditional songs and dances of his homeland were probably doomed to extinction by social change, he spent the rest of his life seeking and preserving them — not only in Britain but among American families with British roots. Eventually he became known as the founding father of England's early twentieth-century folklore revival, and he was a major influence in the creation of the English Folk Dance Society in London and the Country Dance Society in New York — both of which were later to attract Jack Langstaff.

Sharp came three times to clamber for months around remote parts of the Appalachian Mountains with his collaborator Maud Karpeles, collecting songs from the descendants of English, Scottish, and Welsh settlers. They were following in the footsteps of the American folklorist Olive Dame Campbell, and they were just in time, before the tunes of radio and television came creeping in like invasive plants to smother inherited music. "It would often happen that we would hear a voice in the distance," wrote Maud Karpeles afterward, "and then, following it up, we would find, perhaps, a man singing as he hoed his corn patch, or a girl milking a cow, or a woman nursing her baby." They found more than 1,600 songs, some of them early versions that had not only crossed the Atlantic with their immigrant singers, but had already died out in the parts of Britain from which they came.

Whether or not Jack had taken Sharp's *English Folk Songs from the Southern Appalachians* from his father's bookshelves, he was about to have a life-changing folk song moment of his own. His young teacher Carol Preston was not only a member of the Country Dance Society but was living with two other country dancers, one of them an English-born dancing teacher, May Gadd, who would shortly become the society's national director. May Gadd, often known simply as "Gay," was more interested in dance than song, but both she and Carol were steeped in the old tunes inherited from the British Isles. It's possible that these two enlisted Jack for a CDS performance in New York while he was still a soprano; he had a vague memory of having first played and sung the part of St. George in a Mummers' Play when he was thirteen. At any rate, in the summer of 1936 Carol convinced Esther and Meredith to let her take Jack down to a major folk song event, the White Top Folk Festival in Marion, Virginia. Jack was fifteen. His voice was changing, his choirboy days were over; this year, Ken and Dave would be the only Langstaff sopranos at Bretton Woods.

So off went Jack with Miss Preston, in a car with problems; they had frequent flat tires and very dim lights, as Jack reported home, "so we have to go slow at night." He found that you could get a driver's license in Virginia if you were over fourteen, and he contemplated doing that, but not for long.

The car is very funny, we are going along smooth and nicely, when all of a sudden it just splutters and stops! And in a few minutes it starts up again; we don't know what it is. . . . I don't think I will try to get a license (I am a bit slow on shifting gears and remembering about putting on and off the clutch when doing so).

For a fifteen-year-old New Englander the trip southward was full of discovery; he saw his first Civil War battleground and found himself soloist at a Virginia church service, singing an unaccompanied solo of "Abide with Me" just before the Benediction. He also did so much horseback riding that for a while he had to eat all his meals, and write his letters home, standing up.

We have been staying at a very big old place called Gaymont, the beds are great big four-posters and are made of hard, heavy wood but they have no mattresses so it is very uncomfortable. It is so old that there are no bathtubs or any running water, so we fetch water from the well and wash in china basins. What a life! I am as red as a beet. What a sunburn. The milk I drink is just like our thick cream in the city. Miss Preston bought me two swell pairs of white ducks as a present, I didn't want her to do it but you know her. I have met a lot of nice boys and <u>girls</u>. (In fact we are going to spend a whole week in a <u>girls' camp</u>. That's pretty bad.) Boy, is my derriere sore from riding on a horse!

Carol Preston had bought the white pants for Jack because she was about to introduce him to Morris dancing. Once they arrived in Marion, Virginia, he was suddenly in the world of folk song and folk dance.

I am taking the dancing course free from Richard Chase (a swell young man) because one of the young men on the Marion dancing team has died and so Richard wants me to take his place for the big Festival on White Top. Boy! It's hard but it is loads of fun. We do a sword dance and two Morris dances; the Morris dances are the hardest but I think they are swell. I want to show you when I get back home.

*I am taking John Powell's course on folk music which is
fascinating. I have learned all the "Singing Games," "Country
Dances," "Reels," and lots more.*

And at White Top he was astounded by some aged Appalachian
singers performing folk songs passed on from their forebears — a
few of them perhaps the same singers that Cecil Sharp had heard.
His friend Jerry Epstein quoted him later as saying, "At first I could
not imagine that someone with an old cracked voice could get up in
front of people and sing like that. But by the second or third verse I
was hooked."

After White Top, Jack went to a local high school for the next
year. He lived at home in Brooklyn, marinated in other kinds of
music than folk song.

*We didn't have any money but my mother was amazing; all
these musicians would come to the house. The whole renaissance of early music was starting then. I remember Dolmetsch
came to New York, and the English singers the Friends of
Music sang madrigals at Town Hall — they came to the
house. . . . Wanda Landowska the great harpsichordist . . .
Thurston Dart . . . And sometimes, Carol Preston would say,
"Let's go and hear some Wagner," and we heard Flagstad
at the Met, and Richard Crooks, and Björling . . . we never
bought a ticket, we'd stand, and wait until there was an
empty seat.*

By June of 1937 he was back with folk music, working as a
waiter — and singing and dancing — on his first visit to Pinewoods
Camp in Plymouth, Massachusetts, where the Country Dance
Society had thriving summer programs. Cecil Sharp's English Folk

Dance Society in the U.K., the parent organization of the American CDS, was now run by Douglas Kennedy; he had not only taken it over from Sharp and merged song with dance (turning it into the English Folk Dance and Song Society) but was married to Helen Karpeles, sister of Sharp's fellow collector Maud. Kennedy visited Pinewoods regularly.

Into this small, ebullient world came sixteen-year-old Jack Langstaff, talented, enthusiastic, lean, dark, and handsome, and met someone who was later to become an even closer mentor than Carol Preston. "Douglas Kennedy arrived today," he wrote home. "He is a grand person and knows his stuff!" And the next day, as he wrote decades later for an English folk song magazine, he heard Kennedy sing.

I heard him sing English folk songs and ballads, informally and unaccompanied, which made a lasting impression on me. . . . Douglas Kennedy's way with a song was to become my model for the "revival" singer of folk song.

From this point on, folk song had a permanent place in Jack's musical life, though his classical training took precedence. Back at home in the fall, he reported in a letter to Ken — now in his second year at Choate — that he was off for his first madrigal night with their parents ("I will sing bass!"), and that he was about to start lessons with their uncle Arthur, the Wagnerian tenor. Arthur Geary had been keeping a wary eye on the development of Jack's vocal cords; when the voice had begun changing from soprano to alto, he had advised Esther that Jack's lucrative appearances as a boy soloist should stop.

In the winter of 1937, the Langstaff parents went to Palm Beach, leaving Jack, at seventeen, in nominal charge of the household.

He wrote to them that he was "good and sore" at twelve-year-old David for putting on a loud jazz record while the radio was playing *Parsifal,* and added cheerfully that "the first night you weren't here I left all the lights on in the halls overnight! Well! Live and Learn."

At the same time, fifteen-year-old Ken wrote to his parents from Choate.

I only wish I could be home when you're away, because with Jack in charge (only) anything in this world may happen. Do tell him to be careful and all.

Esther's letter books record no warnings or reports of disaster, however, probably because she and Meredith knew very well that affairs at 39 Garden Place were actually run by their indispensable cook-housekeeper, Albertine, known as Allie.

Eventually, after a crash course at summer school, Jack joined his younger brother at Choate. Now he was singing the baritone parts in the headmaster's beloved Gilbert and Sullivan: the Pirate King in *The Pirates of Penzance,* Roderic in *Ruddigore.* Choate was a markedly conservative Yankee school, with no Jews and not many Catholics (though the Kennedy boys made it, and JFK graduated in 1935). But Jack admired the headmaster, George St. John:

He was a remarkable man, he had a sense of the things that were important. He'd say grace to all five hundred of us at breakfast, and on some gorgeous spring day he would then say, "I will lift up mine eyes—" and a great shout would go up, because it meant that the whole school would go outdoors to the top of the hill, and there would be trucks up there waiting with our food.

32

Finding that he was in theory thirty pounds underweight for his height, Jack went out for crew, though this didn't last. Ken reported home that his brother was "doing surprisingly well in his studies." Jack himself reported, "We are all run like a machine and there is too damn much organization!" But if Esther's letter books are to be trusted (she kept, after all, only the letters she wanted to keep), he had a remarkably sunny adolescence, both at Choate and out of it. He sang, he acted, he worked, he played, and by the time he was writing home with plans for a benefit concert his mother was organizing for April 1939, he was edging toward the shape of the recitals he was to give years later as a professional singer.

If I don't try to do a program "over my head" it might work out well enough. I will go ahead, at any rate, with working on some G and S, some oratorio, folk songs, and light concert material here at school, so as to have some kind of a ready repertoire from which you can pick when I get back home. . . . I should like to keep my end of the concert a bit informal, at least to be able to say a few words here and there explaining the lighter folk songs.

And although both boys frequently acknowledged the need to be frugal, their life can't have lacked for much. In one letter Ken, after assuring his mother that money from home was spent on "wholesome cookies, not the rich and filling kind," wrote this:

What I especially want for my birthday! To have my tails coat refaced with the same kind of silk that is on it now. And also have the buttons that are on it now, taken off and buttons like Daddy's put on. The present buttons are much too far out of date.

As Roderic in *Ruddigore,* Jack wore "an all bright, shimmering costume of gold with enormous dark-green cloak fastened to the length of my arm and legs in bat-like style." Ken wrote, "Jack is sensational . . . he gives it a little grand opera with his gorgeous voice and tones and resonance." Their parents came to the performance and — to Jack's great pleasure — brought small Esther. "Now," he wrote, "we'll have to see if Allie can't make it sometime."

He never stopped performing. In the spring he went to visit Carol Preston, who had been made headmistress of the Potomac School, near Washington, D.C., and he shared a room with Douglas Kennedy and was taught the dances needed as demonstration for a lecture Kennedy gave on folk dance. As he told a folk song magazine later, this had the same mesmerizing effect on him as hearing Kennedy sing.

I shall never forget watching that tall lively man dance the Morris jigs with such marvelous lift and infectious rhythm. He taught us that movement stemmed from the dancer's organic being, centered in the solar plexus and radiating out from that center of energy to the extremities of the limbs and to the top of one's head. I remember thinking that Mr. Kennedy had an almost animalistic approach to movement. Although he could be aesthetically demanding of his dancers and singers in the display performances for which he was a master of "choreography" (as I remember so vividly in the Albert Hall productions he later directed), he had a way of encouraging us as novice dancers to be natural and spontaneous.

But folk song and folk dance were still only a part of Jack's life. A month or two later he sang the bass/soprano duet from the Bach cantata *Wachet Auf* with a visiting soprano in the Choate Chapel. Ken turned the pages. "His recitative is gorgeous and his German beautiful, you'd have loved it," he reported home.

An outstanding boy soprano does not necessarily find himself with a wonderful adult voice, but at eighteen Jack was drawing as much attention as he had at eight. When Choate joined forces with several other schools for a concert at the enormous Bushnell Hall in Hartford, Connecticut, he was the star of the evening. And his instincts as a performer took care of him even before a packed house of 2,800.

I was unusually nervous right up till the time I hit the stage. As soon as I stepped on the stage I felt the audience, and the voice came through for me in good style. My nervousness left me as I sensed the audience. They seemed to like it and I got three or four — I can't remember it all now — lengthy curtain calls which was the most appreciative thing I heard that evening. It was after "Jeannie" that I let the voice out in the chorus numbers, much to the surprise of some of the boys from other schools about me.

He was drawing attention in other areas as well; later that term he wrote home from Choate:

It seems that Howard Hughes is going to return to films again as a promoter and producer in his own company; for he had a couple of scouts appear the other day to interview Elebash and me at Mr. Ryan's recommendation. The man took about twenty-four pictures of me around the campus; I sang; he asked questions and I am still in the dark as to what it is all about. At any rate, don't get excited. I'm not!

By summer of 1939 this hint of a Hollywood future had evaporated, mercifully, and all three Langstaff boys were back at Bretton Woods for the last time, helping to supervise the youngest boys and singing in all the concerts. They even still did the "Three Little Maids" trio from *The Mikado,* with Jack presumably singing falsetto. He still enjoyed the camp and its White Mountain audiences, but his tolerance for the concerts' musical content was rapidly going downhill.

As the time draws near for you to hear the concert program, I get even more so disgusted with it. Some of the numbers are truly good, nearly all are done well, and the chorus sounds quite well; but some of the <u>junk</u> and <u>slop</u> that is done is downright embarrassing at times.

And while he sang, he was very much aware of what was happening across the Atlantic, as Hitler groped at Europe, and the British prime minister Neville Chamberlain desperately tried to avoid declaring war.

We had the biggest congregation at our church today. All the seats were taken, extra seats too; people lined the aisles, and sat on the lowest part of the altar. I even had two women sitting next to me in my choir pew! I suppose it was the war scare that brought them, and I think we can all understand that. I've made up my mind what I shall do in case the U.S. is drawn into the conflict, and I only hope K. and D. can join me if possible.

CHAPTER THREE

"THE NEWS SEEMS TO GET
WORSE AND WORSE."

*A*fter the last summer at Bretton Woods, Jack had to make up some academic leeway; he was almost nineteen years old, but for most of those years he had spent more time singing than studying anything unrelated to song. Back he went to Choate as a sixth-former, struggling with subjects like biology ("the most impossible and boring of subjects to understand") and making music with an unspecified "group," which sounds like an early dry run for the Revels.

I teach them "rounds," folk songs, sea chanteys, spirituals, and always end with a hymn. I always arrange beforehand to have one of the fellows talented along some line, to perform a piece or so, and then the rest of the time is for the "making of music" with our combined voices. It is truly wonderful — we do a lot of singing — and the boys and masters in it, love it.

By 1940 World War II was raging in Europe, but the United States was still in its lull before the storm. Jack's letters home dealt mainly with performing, schoolwork, and sometimes girls. ("Steele won't let Ken and me go to the senior dance down at Dobbs on the second because it's too near exams! He is the one master in school whom I *can't stand.*") He was "not actually sure in my mind" that he wanted to go on to four years of college work. He played the Pirate King in *The Pirates of Penzance* ("Boy, do I tingle with excitement during the playing of the overture!"), and after dragging his feet for a while, he followed the example of his two younger brothers and was confirmed into the Episcopal Church.

Younger brother Ken, more successful at schoolwork, was now headed for Harvard, on scholarship. Jack would have to go back to Choate. He spent part of the summer of 1940 with David at the Pinewoods Camp near Plymouth, Massachusetts, for its Country Dance Society summer session; they washed windows and cleared the grounds, as part of the cleanup team before the camp opened. By now the wide Langstaff network of friends included not only Carol Preston, May Gadd, and Douglas Kennedy but most of the major names of the early folk-dance movement, including Helen Storrow, who had founded Pinewoods, and the Conant family, to whom she left it when she died. At some point, Jack recalled later, May Gadd involved him in a folk-dance program for the early days of television. "I had to sing some songs in the first television studio in New York, in Grand Central Station, very primitive. I can't imagine who saw it."

More momentous in his own view was a recital that he regarded as his first real concert, initiated perhaps by his mother. "It was in a hall in Brooklyn — I sang some opera, this and that. We did it as a benefit for the Met, and raised maybe four hundred dollars. I had a young accompanist called Duncan Phyfe, who later on became head of music at Choate. And I got a review in the *Journal-American,* whose headline read, 'A Singer to the Manner Born.' I was nineteen years old, and that meant a lot to me."

Back at Choate, he ran the Glee Club and started to learn the piano, with an eye to music school entrance. The family carol party was the peak of Christmas 1940, though the three attractive Langstaff sons all had a crowded New York social life. Jack wrote home, "It doesn't look as if I will have any evenings at all with you at home, if I accept many of these stupid deb invitations." Ken listed eight dates for dinners and dances in as many days, and even fifteen-year-old David had a dinner-dance invitation, from another fifteen-year-old, Diane Guggenheim.

Then Jack sent in his application for the Curtis Institute of Music, in Philadelphia — with some misgivings, since he had much admired its president, the composer Randall Thompson, who had recently been fired. Then as now, Curtis was remarkable not just for the quality of its teachers but for providing every accepted student with free tuition. Jack was given an audition, at which he sang one piece from Handel's *Messiah* — and "I got in, which was amazing."

Large dark clouds were looming over this tranquil world of music and dancing in the summer of 1941, and he tried not to look at them.

The news seems to get worse and worse each hour with amazing horror. I don't see how France is going to hold out much longer, and I have finally gotten to the point, myself, where I purposely avoid the news comments broadcasted each evening because of the inevitable cowardice it makes me feel for our own country's actions.

In August he went on his first miniature tour, giving seven recitals of songs in assorted Vermont camps and houses, with David as accompanist. Then off he went to Philadelphia, to settle himself for his studies at Curtis. His mother went with him.

"She helped me find somewhere to live—a little room at the top of a dentist's house, for four dollars and fifty cents a week. And because I needed to earn money, we went to four or five churches and I auditioned to sing. The one who took me was in Germantown—'I need a bass,' he said. And my amazing mother said to him, 'We're ten dollars short to get home.' So we borrowed it."

He wrote home, at the beginning:

Start in this Sunday morning at Calvary Church in German-town with "Elijah's" prayer. I have to pay my rent in advance and I don't know when I'll get my first pay (end of the month, I guess). Am having a piano moved into my room here this week—going to cost me $10—but I believe that it is most necessary. . . . I do get a bit lonely once in a while, and find myself wasting precious time by wandering around.

He wasn't lonely for long, of course.

I've got a grand bunch of teachers here at Curtis; Bonelli is my major; Soffray for Solfège and Dictation; Vittorini for Italian language and Italian Renaissance (cultural); Jeanne Behrend for piano; Mme. Gregory for Italian diction; and Westmoreland and Rosenek as two separate coaches every week. . . . I've met some very nice people here in Philly and have had some delightfully enjoyable times. Tonight I dine with Martha Benson who heard me in Manchester this summer, and then to the Symphony with her to hear Rachmaninoff! Drinkers tomorrow evening for music, after luncheon with the Heilners in Chestnut Hill. My job is cer-

tainly going to make life difficult when vacation sets in, and I
find I have to commute! So I'm trying to make it up by pick-
ing up odd jobs here and there; going to try to connect with
the Germantown Symphony and Germantown Youth Sym-
phony Orchestra to see if they would like to hire a young
American baritone as soloist this year; would like to pick up
odd Sunday night or afternoon services here in town; WFIL
offered me a program with small string orchestra (after my
audition for them) to go on the air each week with the kind of
music I would like to do, but — no pay. WCAU promised me
this week that they don't let their artists go unpaid — my
audition for them comes up this coming week.

"Drinkers tomorrow evening for music" was a reference to
Henry Drinker, founder of the Bach Choir, who, Jack said later,
would invite to his house only people who could perform. "I
wasn't so good at sight-reading . . . but one night it would be madrigals, another night people would be there with fiddles for chamber music. . . . He'd say, 'And after supper we'll do the Brahms
Requiem.' He was a terrible conductor, flailing around, like Vaughan
Williams — but wonderful."

By October 1941, he was reporting home from Curtis that he
had some "swell friends."

I'm practically "in love" with my piano teacher, I think, but
I guess I'm also her problem child, at that. Wait till you hear
the amazing tale of how close I came to doing the Messiah
with a big choral society here in town and an orchestra of
over fifty pieces under Nicholas Douty; and how I tried to
learn "Why Do the Nations Rage" in twenty-four hours from
a recording. I think you'll be proud of my brashness! Boy, the

work sure is piling up here, and I feel that unless I'm really
helping to earn my living (in other words, being paid for some
work) that the best return for my investment of time is spent
in working at my studies. That's one reason why I'm not tak-
ing that nonpaying job on the air — and I don't think it's fair
to Bonelli or the Institute for me to take on any work beyond
what's necessary. I'm to appear as soloist with the American
Society of Ancient Instruments on the fourth in the afternoon
at the Ritz-Carlton. English and American folk songs, bal-
lads, carols — with harpsichord accompaniment and dressed
in costume! $25 — not much, but it is a great honor, really
and lucky happening.

His voice teacher at Curtis was the baritone Richard Bonelli,
who was actually born George Richard Bunn, near Syracuse. (Jack
reported that his Wagnerian tenor uncle, Arthur Geary, also suc-
cumbed to this kind of emendation, calling himself Arturo di Geari.)
"Bonelli was great," Jack said, "but sometimes you wouldn't have
a lesson for a few weeks because he was a wonderful baritone and
was singing at the Met. . . . Three times a week I had Leo Rosenek,
a great teacher of German lieder — a little short German, a lovely
man. . . . And the first desk people from the Philadelphia orchestra
were some of the best teachers there. Tabuteau, the great oboist, he
had the Curtis orchestra and conducted it every week. He'd lock the
hall, but I'd go in half an hour early and lie down under the seats at
the back. He was brutal, he'd tear someone down every time, but he
was wonderful, his phrasing. . . . I heard everything he said about
phrasing, and he was a tremendous influence on me without anyone
knowing."

His piano teacher, Jeanne Behrend, was a tremendous influence too; indeed, she was his first lover. "I was a terrible piano

student. . . . She lived across the street from me. I was nineteen and she was in her thirties, but she looked younger. . . . I fell madly in love with her. She'd been married to a pianist, but he was manic-depressive and he'd committed suicide. Alfred Mann was a friend of hers, and John Edmunds, and she'd been a classmate of Sam Barber's — she was a real Charles Ives person too; she really got me interested in singing American music. And she wrote me a couple of songs. . . . Jeanne was very important in my life, a great friend. And then the war broke out."

In his early years at Choate, Jack had felt he was a pacifist ("I remember passing out leaflets at a rally at Madison Square Garden where Paul Robeson spoke"), but that had long been overtaken by his conviction that he and his country should no longer stay apart from the conflict raging in Europe. Now, suddenly, the world changed. On December 8, 1941, along with most other Americans, he listened to President Roosevelt's address to the nation after the Japanese bombed Pearl Harbor. The speech took six minutes.

Mr. Vice President, Mr. Speaker, members of the Senate and the House of Representatives:

Yesterday, December 7, 1941 — a date which will live in infamy — the United States of America was suddenly and deliberately attacked by naval and air forces of the Empire of Japan.

The United States was at peace with that nation, and, at the solicitation of Japan, was still in conversation with its government and its emperor looking toward the maintenance of peace in the Pacific. Indeed, one hour after Japanese air squadrons had commenced bombing in the American island of Oahu, the Japanese ambassador to the United States and his colleague delivered to our secretary of state a formal reply to a recent American message. And while this reply stated that it seemed useless to continue the existing diplomatic negotiations, it contained no threat or hint of war or of armed attack.

It will be recorded that the distance of Hawaii from Japan makes it obvious that the attack was deliberately planned many days or even weeks ago. During the intervening time the Japanese government has deliberately sought to deceive the United States by false statements and expressions of hope for continued peace.

The attack yesterday on the Hawaiian Islands has caused severe damage to American naval and military forces. I regret to tell you that very many American lives have been lost. In addition, American ships have been reported torpedoed on the high seas between San Francisco and Honolulu.

Yesterday the Japanese government also launched an attack against Malaya.

Last night Japanese forces attacked Hong Kong.

Last night Japanese forces attacked Guam.

Last night Japanese forces attacked the Philippine Islands.

Last night the Japanese attacked Wake Island.

And this morning the Japanese attacked Midway Island.

Japan has, therefore, undertaken a surprise offensive extending throughout the Pacific area. The facts of yesterday and today speak for themselves. The people of the United States have already formed their opinions and well understand the implications to the very life and safety of our nation.

As commander in chief of the Army and Navy, I have directed that all measures be taken for our defense.

But always will our whole nation remember the character of the onslaught against us. No matter how long it may take us to overcome this premeditated invasion, the American people in their righteous might will win through to absolute victory.

I believe that I interpret the will of the Congress and of the people when I assert that we will not only defend ourselves to the uttermost but will make it very certain that this form of treachery shall never again endanger us.

Hostilities exist. There is no blinking at the fact that our people, our territory, and our interests are in grave danger.

With confidence in our armed forces — with the unbounding determination of our people — we will gain the inevitable triumph — so help us God.

I ask that the Congress declare that since the unprovoked and dastardly attack by Japan on Sunday, December 7, 1941, a state of war has existed between the United States and the Japanese Empire.

With FDR's voice still in his ears, Jack called his father and announced that he was going to enlist in the Army. "In my ignorance, I thought it would all be over in two or three months. I knew Dad would have disapproved if I'd been a conscientious objector — he'd been in the infantry in World War I. So I called him. And he said, 'Can't you come back first for the carol party?'"

Meredith himself was chafing to get back into uniform, in Washington, D.C. ("Why can't General Osborn or General Marshall put me in a colonel's uniform and let me smash into some real constructive work?") Four days after FDR's speech, Germany declared war on the U.S., and the conflict officially became worldwide. Jack wrote to his father in D.C. on December 16:

Dear Dad:

In your questioning there in Washington of the right thing for me to do at this time, will you please look into the possibility for some work in the Army along the lines in which I might be most helpful and fitted.

In the two recent contacts I have had with singing for (entertaining) the men — at Fort Hancock and Dix — I can see the kind of relaxation through music they need, as well as discovering the great importance of getting soldiers to sing forth vigorously at such occasions, when I've had the chance to get 'em going with informal leadership.

Couldn't a unit of us go forth from Curtis to give all the camps some of that, through informal, light music — yet of a good standard? It amazes me the amount of amateur (? — no, mediocre!) entertainment that gets into those camps. I've seen it, and I know that that sort of thing is no more appreciated by the soldier than it would be by anybody else.

There is a splendid group of us here who would like to help in that way, if it's possible.

Anyway, I'm waiting until after Xmas, but convinced that I must do something, and finding it hellish to just sit around and wait like this.

So he went home to Brooklyn Heights for the family Christmas, and then he joined the U.S. Army.

Chapter Four

—————

"Things go deep with him."

*T*he Army sent Jack to Fort Hancock, out on the spit called Sandy Hook off the coast of New Jersey; he had visited it a few months earlier as a singer, entertaining the men. This time he was one of them. In Esther Langstaff's letter book there's a copy of a letter from the Office of the Harbor Defense Commander at Fort Hancock headed "Enlistment of Mr. Jack Langstaff." It reads:

At the present time a vacancy exists in the Office of the Morale Officer at this station.

Mr. Langstaff's unusual training makes him admirably suited to fill this vacancy.

In view of the suitability of this man, it is desirable to fill this vacancy immediately in lieu of waiting for a suitable replacement.

I accept the responsibility for the recruit training of this man.

Signed: P. S. Gage,

Brigadier General, U.S. Army, Commanding

"I was a sad sack in the Army," said Jack. "I didn't know anything about anything. They didn't have a uniform that would fit me, so I started off in a long greatcoat from World War I. Dropped my machine gun in the sand, the sergeant gave me hell."

But in no time he had found the makings of a Glee Club among the recruits sharing his basic training. "I got thirty-five or so of them together who liked to sing, and I taught them all kinds — the Dartmouth drinking song, *Porgy and Bess,* sea chanteys, even the Boyce *Alleluia.* They just loved it, that sound — we'd be drinking beer in the PX and they'd say, 'Let's do the *Alleluia.*'"

Soon his Fort Hancock Glee Club was giving concerts, and Jeanne Behrend came to join one of them, as guest artist.

Jack's indomitable mother, Esther, came down to visit him at the camp as well. According to his memory later, she contrived to meet his commanding officer, General Gage, and completely charmed him. "She said, 'Oh, General, I do like those things on your shoulder; I wonder if Jack will ever get some?' He was very taken with her — later on, Allie told me, he turned up at our Brooklyn house in a car with flags on it to take her out to lunch."

Esther's instinct for nudging along the course of Jack's life was not daunted by the fact that he was now in the Army. Before long she was back again, joining his singing soldiers at a concert as accompanist. She wrote home: "Jack and I called on his nibs the general and he was most cordial and very nice to us. Oh, by the way, Jack came up before the Officers Board last week and evidently they thought very well of him . . . then I went down again yesterday afternoon and I called on Mrs. Gage and we two gals had several martinis that she certainly knows how to make . . . then I returned to the Gages' for dinner and he was there and we are all very chummy now and they both call me Esther!"

And in April she came back yet again, accompanying Jack at a recital in a high-school auditorium in Fredonia, New York. She wrote to Meredith that Jack had been a great success. "He, of course, thought he didn't do so well. But then he *always* thinks that!"

Esther Langstaff, as Jack once said, would have made a wonderful manager. She certainly appears to have been the manager of the Langstaff family, unchallenged until the children grew to an age to contemplate their own unquestioning adoration. In a letter to her from Harvard that summer, Ken wrote about having realized "what an abnormally high-pitched, going-every-minute life" the family had led. "You brought us up the way you did, because your character is that way — it's driving and impetuous seasoned with clever and invaluable foresight." He then cautioned her to be more sympathetic to young Esther, later known as Terry, who was the only Langstaff left at home, the daughter who probably suffered from coming after the three beautiful, talented boys.

"The fluctuations between hot and cold, harshness and sweetness, in your personality are really too much for one to stand and develop normally," wrote Ken. "Reason it for yourself — you'll see it's true, and Esther will be only too willing to play the game with you — she's got a level head and can understand."

"Terry got short shrift from my mother," Jack said once. "She used to call her the dividend. 'I've got three boys — oh, and a daughter.'"

But the eldest of the three boys had spun out of his mother's orbit now. Esther was a persuasive and persistent lady, and Jack inherited and employed those same gifts tirelessly in later years, but

49

from this point on even she could no longer influence his life. He was a soldier. In August 1942 he went to Infantry Officer Training School in Fort Benning, Georgia, and there were far fewer mentions of singing in his letters home. Music was overtaken by the need to learn other skills, like digging foxholes and using a bayonet.

Three months later he graduated as "marksman" with an M1 rifle, "second-class gunman" with a heavy machine gun, "expert" with a light machine gun. He wrote to his father that he failed to make "sharpshooter" with the M1 because he had been hungover that morning on the range. At twenty-one, he was — like most Americans and all Europeans in 1942 — facing the hardest time of his life. His company commander told him he was one of the youngest, most inexperienced, and most sheltered of all the men there. Jack wrote home that he felt he needed "more of a *display* of forcefulness in my leadership."

He graduated, in due course, and after a visit home he was flown across the country to Camp Roberts in California, north of San Luis Obispo, where he would teach recruits. In a bare tree outside the camp he found mistletoe growing; he climbed up and picked some, and mailed it home for the Christmas carol party.

On Christmas Eve 1942, his twenty-second birthday, he went to the post's Field Artillery Chapel and led the Carol Sing after the midnight service: "And was I pleased," he wrote, "to find some of the soldiers calling out for such as 'Greensleeves' and 'In Dulci Jubilo' among their requests for favorites."

The comment on his sheltered background bothered him: how could he forearm the brothers who had shared that background, and who would soon face this drastically altered future? On Christmas Day 1942 he began writing an earnest letter: "To my dear brothers: It has been long my intention to write you both now that you are about to join us in the service."

Then he was interrupted, and broke off. But when Ken and David were really on the brink of joining the army a month later, he became even more anxious to try to warn them what to expect, and he sat down to finish his letter on the night of January 25, 1943.

Jack wrote that he was duty officer that evening, appointed to make hourly inspections of the whole camp until six AM. "The cooks just brought me over a big GI pitcher full of strong coffee and a whole pumpkin pie — both are sitting on the radiator in readiness for my midnight feast!" After this reminder of boarding school, he then tried to explain to his brothers the things that he had learned about, and from, the men in his charge — men who came from the world outside 39 Garden Place, Brooklyn Heights, and whose mothers were not acquainted with musicians or generals.

I have men who don't know or have never learned what it is to take baths and keep themselves clean; good and fine men who have not had any education beyond the second grade (and some of 'em old enough to be my father — think of that, if you will!); men who cannot write their own names but have to make their 'mark'; men who are eating the best food they have ever had in their lives and who are more warmly clad than they were ever able to be before. They are getting a chance, anyway, at a little education . . . they are learning first aid, hygiene, sex hygiene, history, geography, and even courtesy. They are more fit than the day they landed here. . . .

Are not all these things — if we can instill them in these men to last — going to make far better citizens in a future world and give them a chance to raise our country's standards of ethics among a large group of hitherto uneducated people? Mind you, though, when I say 'uneducated' I mean nothing more, for you will find, too, that many of the uneducated have

*a common sense that is far above a lot of us who got ours
out of a book; and you will also find the fine points in simple
people that make them just as loyal and trustworthy as any
former school chum.*

If he had felt his world expanding as a boy when he listened to
"simple people" singing songs inherited from their forebears, he was
learning a great deal more than that in the army. He wasn't about to
reject the virtues of his own privileged background, however. His
letter went on to admonish his brothers not to "degenerate into a
simple and much too limited vocabulary" common in the army, and
to go on reading in their free moments:

*Just remember this, Ken and Dave: don't ever lose your sense
of values — your standards — keep 'em as they are!*

Choose your friends for their humanity, he said to them, not for
their background. You don't have to aim at being an officer.

*But noncom or officer, there are two words, two points that
you will have to bring forcibly to both your characters —
believe me, sincerely, in this — <u>aggressiveness</u> and <u>initiative</u>.*

And after this echo of his company commander, he went on
to make them an impassioned plea for learning, in particular, the
techniques of using the bayonet and the hand grenade —"especially
when you stop to realize what the sword and the knife stand for, in
proficiency, with our slant-eyed enemy."

It was all a very long way from oratorio.

The jarring words "our slant-eyed enemy" were uncharacteristic
of Jack, but they were commonplace in the America of 1943. For

everyone in the United States, Pearl Harbor and its aftermath had demonized everyone and everything connected to Japan; government posters showing grinning, slit-eyed enemy faces were everywhere, and almost 120,000 Americans of Japanese descent were forced into internment camps for the duration of the war. Like most other Americans, Jack recovered from his xenophobia after hostilities were over, though perhaps it's not accidental that his lifelong fascination with the music and folklore of other cultures never made any major connection with the Far East. In January 1943, he was simply intent on being a good American soldier.

So he mailed his long, admonitory letter to his brothers, a month after its interrupted Christmas Day beginning. They knew, by then, the reason for the interruption. Shortly after Christmas, Jack had found himself engaged to be married.

Since his time at Curtis, there had been three romantic interests in Jack's life, all of them to some degree friends of the family. "There was Jeanne, there was Judy Taylor, a wonderful girl I used to dance with, and there was Diane Guggenheim, who was very young. Carol Preston said to me, 'I'm not going to advise you about any one of them.'"

Diane was not only the youngest of the three but clearly the most impulsive. She was eighteen years old and still a high-school student at the Brearley School in New York; Esther's family letter books include, as noted earlier, one from fifteen-year-old Diane inviting Jack's youngest brother, David, to a dance. She also came from the complicated Guggenheim family, and carried more subconscious emotional baggage than Jack may have imagined.

Diane was the daughter of Harry Guggenheim, third-generation patriarch of the rich, beneficent Jewish family whose fortune had come initially from silver and copper mining. The formidable, domineering Harry had degrees from Yale and Cambridge, and was an

53

aviation pioneer and pilot who fought in both world wars. He was also a die-hard Republican, and in 1929 President Hoover appointed him U.S. Ambassador to Cuba for four years. By then Diane, daughter of his second wife, Carol, was four years old. Carol was Caroline Morton Potter, daughter of Theodore Roosevelt's secretary of the Navy, and both she and Harry had divorced their former spouses in order to marry in 1923. They each had two teenage daughters, though the only one of these who had chosen to live with them was Harry's daughter Nancy, nine years older than Diane. Born in 1924, Diane was their only child together.

Diane's childhood, in Cuba and then New York and the family's Long Island mansion, Falaise, was tempestuous; perhaps its only stable point was a beloved Irish nanny better able to show love than her parents were. Her mother, Carol, was dreamy and unstable, drank heavily, and eventually took up with the sin-obsessed, sex-avoiding Moral Rearmament movement of the time. Her half sister Nancy was in a state of constant rebellion against Harry's mania for control — and when Nancy married George Draper in 1939, they moved to California, George said, "To get as far away as we could from our families." The Guggenheim household was not peaceful.

In 1937 Carol left Harry for a New York apartment of her own, taking thirteen-year-old Diane with her. Two years later they were divorced. By then Diane was a day student at the Brearley School (which had declined to admit Harry's older two daughters in 1924 because "the definite quota of Jewish children . . . had been made up for the year"). She was a pretty girl, and loved music, but apparently she made her mother's life so difficult that Harry often had to intervene, even though he was by now involved with Alicia Patterson, the feisty lady who was to become his third wife. Alicia was thirty-one, sixteen years younger than Harry, and beautiful; she had been a reporter, and like him she knew how to hunt, fish, and fly a plane. They married in 1939 as soon as they divorced their second spouses — just as Harry and Carol had done — and flew off in a two-seater plane for their honeymoon. Shortly thereafter, Harry bought a newspaper for Alicia to run, which became *Newsday.* None of this endeared Alicia to his teenage daughter.

Diane bitterly resisted the new marriage, despite calming efforts from her stepsisters, but there was nothing she could do about it. Now she had not only a troubled relationship with her mother but a stepmother whom she deeply resented. It's hard to resist the feeling that Jack, for Diane, was not just a wonderfully attractive young man but also a wonderful chance for escape.

Harry Guggenheim nearly always commanded a family gathering at Christmas, but in 1942 he, like Meredith Langstaff and his sons, was bent on becoming involved in the war. Though he was fifty-two, he managed to reactivate his commission in the naval air arm and was posted to air bases first in Queens and then in New Jersey. This may have been one reason why nobody prevented teenage Diane from flying to San Francisco at Christmas 1942, nominally to visit her half sister Nancy and family in Northern California.

Jack had told his parents that he planned to spend his Christmas leave in San Francisco, 180 miles from his base, and to go to a concert. "Perhaps I can pick up Diane's sister to go with me if she is free." He duly saw Nancy; Nancy called Diane; Diane announced that she was flying out. "What a time we would have, just in case it does work!" Jack wrote home.

They did indeed. As in the case of Meredith and Esther Langstaff twenty-five years earlier, the peril of war is a great promoter of matrimony. Jack and Diane went out together and ended the evening sitting on a bench on Nob Hill, in the little park next to the Pacific Union Club. He proposed, and she accepted him. The next day they came back to the park in the sunshine, took off their shoes and lined them up under the slats of the bench, and took a picture of it.

So Jack was engaged to be married, to an eighteen-year-old high-school girl. He wrote home, "There is much that Diane and I have to learn, that I know. But it is my hope that you will do what you can for her there at home; and so she will come to know our family and the things we love." But this wasn't your average schoolgirl; it was Diane Guggenheim, impulsive by nature and not patient with deprivation. Two weeks later Jack wrote another letter to his parents, long and incoherent, on January 14, 1943.

> *Dearest Mother and Dad:*
>
> *I write you both, at this time, for some immediate advice — perhaps I have no right bothering my own parents with this great problem of mine; but I do want them to be understanding and give me their opinions, anyway.*
>
> *Diane has just called me. I got her call five minutes after I came in from the field this evening at seven. She doesn't want to wait — she wants us to be together <u>now</u>, as soon as possible; certainly before I go overseas. (She wanted to come out here to me <u>immediately!</u>)*

Then he thought aloud for several pages, about whether Diane should finish high school, about where and when they should marry, about money, about how soon he might be able to "get into things *over there.*" And the request for advice had a characteristically disarming finale:

> *Always remembering how my father and mother came to be married — and what they did with their lives, and for us.*

What could be a better, or more inspiring, example for Diane and me?

Please let me hear some word from you immediately.

Faithfully, Your Jack

Esther preserved no words of reply in the letter books, but before long she and Diane had started to plan a huge Guggenheim/Langstaff wedding to be held in Grace Church. They were ambitious, elaborate plans; there might be as many as a thousand guests, with Dr. Bowie conducting the service, Ernest Mitchell at the magnificent organ, and the Wagnerian tenor Uncle Arthur singing with the full boys' choir.

Lt. John Langstaff was still teaching recruits at Camp Roberts, California. In February, he gave an orientation lecture called "Our National Effort 1939–1943" to his entire battalion of a thousand officers and men, and another to the volunteer officer candidates on jungle warfare. Then he was given ten days' leave to go back east and get married.

The big wedding became in the event a small one, since there had been a recent death in the Guggenheim family and it seemed no time for a gala. Dr. Bowie married Jack and Diane in the Grace Church chantry, with young Terry as a bridesmaid, Ken and David as ushers, and Meredith as best man. Harry Guggenheim gave his daughter away. Uncle Arthur didn't sing, but Ernest Mitchell played the big church organ ("which is far better than the pip-squeak organ in the chantry," Esther had written), and they could all hear it through the open chantry doors. The families' joint invitation list of 1,050 had been ferociously cut, since even with standees, the chantry held only 130 people.

Carol Preston wrote to Esther Langstaff, "I do hope and pray that she is just the girl for him, for he is so fine and so loyal that things go deep with him."

Diane left Brearley without graduating and went back to California with Jack, to live in what he described as a "farmhouse" that he had rented in Atascadero, near the camp. By May, she was pregnant. By July, both Ken and David were in the Army, and Jack had a letter from his first commander, General Gage, telling him to be patient even though he was chafing to go and fight. "This is going to be a long war," wrote the general, "especially in the Pacific."

Esther came out to visit, and Jack reported on "a wonderful weekend in Santa Barbara with Mother and Diane." Then he was posted to the Northwest, to the 96th Division based at Fort Lewis. He and Diane had acquired "a wreck of a car" and they drove up through the redwoods to Camp Adair, Oregon, where 75,000 soldiers would be on maneuvers for the next six months before being shipped out to the Pacific.

And Diane Carol Langstaff was born on December 28, 1943, in Medford, Oregon, twenty-three years and four days after her father.

CHAPTER FIVE

———⟨⟩———

"GOD DAMN THIS WAR!"

*B*y June of 1944 Jack was "a rifle platoon leader in a line out-
fit" scheduled to go to Camp Beale, California, and then
overseas. Diane was in New York; she must have brought
the baby—known henceforth as Carol—east from Oregon earlier
in the year. Jack too came to New York in June, for six-month-old
Carol's christening. "Jack looked well though rather thin," Esther
reported in a letter. Then he went back to Camp Beale, north of
Sacramento, California, and was shortly shipped out on a convoy
bound for the war in the Pacific. They were told they were going
to the island of Yap, a Japanese air and naval base in the Caroline
Islands, between the Philippines and Guam.

Whether by design or accident, the family letter books contain,
from this point on, amazingly few references to Jack's wife. Esther
amiably describes washing diapers, and reports on time spent in

Southampton, Long Island, with young Esther, Carol, and Allie. In a sequence of letters to the "Home Front," Jack sends messages to Carol but never to Diane, and even though he must also have been writing Diane regular private letters, the lack of references to her is striking. In July, from a ship "somewhere in the Pacific" he asks Esther to "kiss my little girl good night for me," and she in return sends him a little woolly ear that Carol has pulled off a toy lamb. It's as if Diane had never chosen, or been allowed, to become part of the close, charmed circle of the Langstaff family. Either that, or in the making of the books, much later, she was edited out. She must certainly have been having a difficult time herself, as a nineteen-year-old mother surviving the whirlpool of her own powerful, daunting family.

Alone at night, Jack wrote home from the ship.

I sang over many songs in my mind, as I looked out over the moonlit waters. . . . Then I said my prayers, for you all, and for us all, and then went below to bed — after finishing censoring my men's mail.

He was a second lieutenant now, and on his way to battle. His convoy reached Hawaii, and in September he wrote of having a couple of hours completely to himself, in some remote spot. So he sang. All on his own in the Pacific sunshine, he sang nonstop, for the whole two hours:

. . . folk songs, lieder, oratorio, opera, Gilbert and Sullivan, madrigals, Christmas carols, symphonies, piano concertos, hymns, and scales! It's amazing how much I have forgotten — I who pride myself on never forgetting a song once I've learned it. The voice seems as good as ever, though.

Then they were at sea again. In October they reached their real destination, the Philippines, for the invasion of the mountainous island of Leyte, which would begin the Battle of Leyte Gulf. It was the largest amphibious operation so far in the Pacific, involving 714 ships of the U.S. Seventh Fleet and the Royal Australian Navy, and two corps of the U.S. Sixth Army. Jack was part of the 96th Infantry Division, splashing ashore under fire on the east coast of Leyte, and then struggling through swamps in a three-day battle to capture a hill from which the Japanese were firing on landing craft. He wrote home, from his tent on a cold beach:

I came through the campaign without so much as a serious scratch. . . . The ear of Carol's lamb is still in my first aid kit. Sergeant Maclean, who is now my platoon sergeant, went through the battle with his baby girl's first little shoe tied to the barrel of his rifle. . . .

Disease, however, hit almost as many men in the Pacific as bullets; before long Jack was in a field hospital, first with dysentery and then with yellow jaundice. From his bed he wrote an enormous letter to his brothers, warning them of the horrors and necessities and tactics of jungle war.

Then he was struggling back to his company through the rainy mountains, and writing again in late November from a tent pitched "in soft, odorous mud, ankle deep when it's *not* raining." There were five of them in the tent, with two quarts of 190-proof medicinal alcohol for nightcaps. He reported that he was filthy but "feeling fine," though sickness and casualties had taken thirteen of his platoon of forty-three men. "One of my noncoms was hit in the head by a sniper's bullet yesterday afternoon. Oh, I prayed so for him, as I sat there by him as he was dying."

The conditions gave him tropical ulcers, and a month later he was back in the field hospital, fuming. He spent Christmas there, writing nostalgic images of home, and lists of the people he wanted to remember him.

Last night I dreamed that I had come home at last and found Carol playing on the floor alone — we talked and played together for quite a while there as we got to know each other again — my, she was a big and beautiful girl! I went to the piano and played and sang some scales for the first time in two years, then I called up an excellent firm in town and ordered three cases of the best sparkling burgundy, a hundred champagne glasses, and pounds of shortbread. Carol and I took a cab, picked up all this stuff at the caterer's and went to 39, arriving there at the stoop just as you all were bursting into 'Adeste Fidelis [sic].' We took all the things we had brought for the party in to Allie, and then I went upstairs to join you all in the music by candlelight with little Carol atop my shoulders singing. I cried — and that was the end of it.

He went back into the field with his platoon, holding a mountain pass against Japanese troops trying to retake it. "Leeches *really* give me the willies," he wrote. Asked to sing to the men before an outdoor movie, he sang "By and By" but couldn't remember the words of any other song they called for. He wrote home about the sensation of going over the side of a landing craft under fire; it had something in common with the nervousness before a concert, but, he wrote, "In battle I found my fear took the form of mad anger, usually."

Then jaundice put him back in the Leyte field hospital, so he missed his platoon's next landing craft mission — the invasion of

Okinawa. When the battalion steamed north from the Philippines, Jack was left behind — and he wrote forlornly, "A young lieutenant commissioned in the field has taken over my platoon." But by mid-April of 1945 he too was on a ship, and by May he was in the front lines on Okinawa. "I seem to have a fine full-strength platoon," he wrote more cheerfully. Though May 7 was VE Day, when hostilities ended in Europe, he wrote that Okinawa "is hell — fighting's like 'Europe,' only the Nips don't surrender, at all!"

He was writing, he said, on blank air letter forms they had found "on two Japanese we shot just outside our hole last night."

This campaign has Leyte beat for fierceness and horror. I have the first platoon of K company at present — most of the men are youngsters, willing fellows, just out of IRTC. . . . We have been living in the midst of crackling rifle fire, pounding mortars, and endless whistling and banging of artillery night and day.

And although he was itching from fleas, with the stench of decaying Japanese and American bodies all around him, he wrote from his foxhole about plans for his musical future.

Escamillo in Carmen, *Scarpia in* Tosca, *Valentine in* Faust, *Figaro in* Barber. *I'd like to study them with Stanley Pratt, for dramatics, and with Hans Wohlmuth for dramatics and operatic interpretation; and possibly with Herbert Graf for operatic tradition. Quite an order, eh what? . . . Later, Stanley Pratt would be wonderful for Verdi's Iago and Falstaff. You are right, I do want to work hard to attain a good foundation and the highest quality to my voice and music before launching out publicly. And so the more mature and difficult roles will also come in time, later, the Mozart ones, the Wagnerian — Strauss, and a few others. At the same time I feel that —*

And the letter broke off, who knows why.

A week later, after an attack, he wrote that he was cooking up cereal and a cup of "our old standby Nescafé — let's never have it around again after this." He was longing for the end of the war.

The air smells clearer and fresher than I've smelled for a long time now, this morning — the dead have been pretty well disposed of by bulldozers in this area, and the torrential rains must have washed the stench away. This cool morning freshness makes me homesick for the hills of Choate.

By early June 1945 he had twenty-six men left in his platoon, out of forty-one. He wrote home from the ruins of a farmhouse, in whose shelter they were making some coffee until dusk, when they would stand guard in their foxholes up the hill. They had just performed a mercy killing.

When we got here this afternoon I found a small Okinawan child (about nine or ten) lying under a blanket, wounded, in a thatched-roof manger, with only a couple of scrawny, crying goats with him. He had a very deep and serious shrapnel wound in his chest and in his leg — must have lain there, all alone, for a couple of days, because gangrene had set in, and the open wounds were crawling with maggots. . . . He was so pathetic and helpless looking, as I stared down at him, that my blood boiled to see what the waging of war did to innocent children — no matter what race. I opened my biscuit can and fed him the crackers and candy; he looked so grateful for it; then I couldn't understand what he was trying to tell me in a weak foreign whisper, until he kept looking toward an old wooden gourd hanging in the straw, and opening and closing his parched lips; I took the ladle, and got him water from the nearby well — not a whimper did he make, so we felt morphine was unnecessary. Our battalion aid station was about two miles to our rear still, and it was impossible to get him back then, for sniper fire was still covering the area we had had to dash across — and so I didn't want to endanger any man's life. He got pretty bad this evening, just as we were about to try to get him back to the medico — we had done all we could, put some sulpha powder about the openings, and applied sterile dressings; but there was no hope, as he suddenly grew much worse. We have just finished him off with a double dose of morphine — he is in a sound and final sleep, and out of his misery. Poor child! — God damn this war!

A week later he wrote a letter mixing anguish and trivia in the way that is produced only by war.

The men are all feeling pretty low today — we were in a hell of a position last night, out in front, and after the perimeter was set in, I gave orders to stay put and fire at anything that moved; we got quite a handful of Japs during the night, but three of my men got a little careless in their foxhole, I guess, and one of our own men shot at them — killing two of the boys, outright, and wounding the other in the neck. It is one of those tragic things; and although it quite upsets us for a while, the man that did the shooting is in no way to blame (I've had a terrible time with him today, he is so broken up over it.)

Don't you think Ken resembles General Eisenhower in this snapshot—not very good of Carol though. I wonder if you could get me a jacket like Ken's; we have not been issued them over here, they must be quite comfortable.

This was his last letter from the front. The next day, being a good soldier, he did something he had warned Ken and David never to do. ("Remember, a platoon commander is not there to do the job of a scout—one of our own officers got it between the eyes, when he left his men, and went out ahead to do some scouting.") Apparently a superior officer was visiting the platoon under Jack's command and wanted an overview of the field. This didn't seem a good idea, but you don't argue with a superior, so out they went, and Jack was shot.

He nearly died. The bullet smashed through his shoulder blade into the chest cavity and through a lung, breaking six ribs and embedding bone fragments in the other lung. He lost a lot of blood. In the field hospital he was set down among the cases that seemed hopeless, but a doctor named Gaynor had him moved, feeling he could be saved. A week later Jack dictated a letter for his family at the hospital; characteristically, he tried so hard to reassure them that for months they had no real idea of the severity of his wound.

I am unable to write at this time so one of the Red Cross workers has been kind enough to help me out.

On June 16, just a few days before the conclusion of our campaign a Jap 90 Mortar sailed into me and here I am in a field hospital.

The War Dept. may notify you so I am writing you so you'll have no anxiety.

My shoulder was broken. I banged up a few ribs, they have me in good care, but life is terribly boring.

Apart from the fact that his wound had been caused by a gunshot, not a mortar shell, the most notable thing about this description is its extreme understatement. In the first weeks after he was shot, the complications of his massive chest wound were kept in check largely by the efforts of Dr. Gaynor, who had rescued him the first day and who turned out to be a chest specialist. ("A fine chap and a crackerjack doctor," Jack said.) He ran a high fever, and the infection was hard to control.

My deepest difficulty is trying to sleep at night—I try to think of pleasant things—going home, playing with little Carol, of refreshing baths or a comfortable bed, New England, the music I will do, of good food (cold), but all I do is have half-awake nightmares, of Okinawa all over again.

But he had on his side, as he had written home earlier in the campaign, "my determination, my enthusiasm, and my faith in God — and my will to live!" Gaynor wanted to send him to a notable chest surgeon named Woodruff, who was at the General Hospital on Guam, 1,400 miles away, but the Air Corps had a rule against carrying chest patients. So Jack had to be put into a large "traveling cast" and shipped in the hot, swaying sick bay of a troop transport to Guam. Major Woodruff, like Gaynor, was the right person in the right place at the right time.

I am very keen about him as a doctor and have complete confidence in him. As a person he is a fine fellow and a real gentleman — a little older than Capt. Gaynor was. He took me right in hand, had them remove the clumsy and tight heavy cast, which enveloped the entire upper part of my body, and put my broken arm in a much more simple, light, and comfortable brace. Then a few days ago he operated on me, removing one rib and draining out a tremendous amount of pus and accumulation from the lung and chest cavity. Then he inserted a rubber tube through my back, into the chest cavity, so now whatever is left in there is slowly draining out day and night through this hose.

He was still being fed intravenously and had been given transfusions of eleven pints of blood; he weighed less than a hundred pounds. Soon he was back in another large cast. "It would be wiser for you not to bring Carol to see me when you come to visit me for the first time in the hospital," he wrote, or rather, dictated.

He added hopefully that his vocal cords were fine. "But it will take a little time for the right lung to expand to its full natural capacity." His mother, busy with travel and still not fully informed, wrote to him, "I understand you are still 'flat on your back.' That must be exceedingly tiresome for you, dear. I hope by now you are raised up a little." Ken, who had only just managed to have the Army send him overseas, flew to Guam to visit Jack, and at first barely recognized him.

Eventually, at the end of September 1945 — after the dropping of what he called "this diabolical atomic weapon" and the end of World War II — Jack was flown via California to Walter Reed Hospital, where he would have several more operations. While he was in California, he did something to prove that whether or not his wife figured in his letters to his family, she was certainly still very much present in his heart, his mind, and his life.

In his brief pause in California, he wrote to the Pacific Union Club on Nob Hill in San Francisco. His letter, and its result, was reported in a news magazine two or three weeks later, on October 15, 1945 — and the magazine found it so touching that the story was plucked from the archives and reprinted in 2006. In the original issue, the correspondent wrote that Jack sent his letter in "late September, 1945, from the debarkation hospital at Hamilton Field." He then described the moment two years earlier when Jack proposed to Diane — who is not named — on the Nob Hill park bench, and the photograph they subsequently took of the bench with their shoes lined up beneath it. After that, he went on to report most of the contents of Jack's letter, and the effect that it had on the recipients.

It read: "Dear Sir: This letter may seem to hold . . . a strange request . . . but I am in earnest. I am an infantry line officer . . . wounded at Okinawa. I am anxious to buy one of the green benches in . . . the little park adjoining the . . . club. A couple of years ago I became engaged to a New York girl one evening while sitting on [it]. We were later married and before I went overseas I . . . got to know a small daughter. I have always promised myself that I would try to get the bench for our garden in our home in New York. I hope you understand . . . John Langstaff, 1st Lieut., Infantry."

Enclosed was a sketch of the park, an X designating the bench.

Transactions of this nature are seldom handled in the Pacific Union Club. And anyhow, the park belongs to the city. Nevertheless the club's manager asked club member Lewis Lapham, the mayor's son, to do something about it. Lapham took the letter to the city Park Commission.

The commissioners engaged in a decent interval of protest and speech. Finally, beaming, they agreed to send the bench, and even (despite Langstaff's insistence on paying for it) to give it and pay the cost of shipping themselves. Then they discovered that the bench had been removed from the park. They organized a search, discovered it, among some discarded machinery, in Golden Gate Park.

Last week, disassembled and crated, it was on its way east to be installed in Lieut. Langstaff's tiny yard on Manhattan's East 62nd Street. And in both the Pacific Union Club and the City Hall a casual visitor might have been puzzled to observe a fleeting and apparently inexplicable smile on the faces of some solid, civic, and all-too-graying men.

It's a most endearing story, particularly if it all happened in the reported time frame of two or three weeks. In Esther Langstaff's letter books, which often included family memorabilia as well as letters, there is, however, no mention of it, nor indeed any reference to the fact that Jack and his wife and daughter had a house in New York. There is only an account of the Langstaff family's traditional Christmas carol party for 1945, written by Esther to Ken and David, who were both still away in the Army. After three months in Walter Reed Hospital, Jack had been allowed to go to New York for Christmas. If Diane and small Carol Langstaff were there in Brooklyn Heights at the party, they are not mentioned.

Jack, Marshall, and John Woodbridge arrived in Carol Morton's car . . . Jack in ribbons and uniform. . . . He sat during all the singing until he came to the final one, which he sang over by the harp, and it was unbelievably beautiful and moving and his voice was very firm, clear, and resonant and he did look so darling, standing up there and looking out over us all.

CHAPTER SIX

"HE HAS TIME TO BECOME AN
OUTSTANDING SINGER."

A surviving 1945 Christmas card from Jack, Diane, and
Carol Langstaff, at 244 East 62nd Street, New York, is
inscribed "Christmas Eve together, 1945." It has a photograph of toddler Carol in her pajamas, gazing pensively into an
open fire above which hang a man's dark sock, a woman's silk stock-
ing, and a little white sock. But the three of them can't have been
together for long, since Jack had been released from Walter Reed
Hospital only for two weeks, and went back to D.C. on January 6,
1946. Though he had sung at the Christmas party, he said later, he'd
had to breathe after every two measures.

Altogether he was in Walter Reed for about a year, for a
sequence of operations. They told him afterward that he might not
have recovered so well if his lungs hadn't been abnormally devel-
oped, from his life as a singer — so it was his dedication to his voice

that brought the voice back to him. His marriage, however, didn't survive.

It's impossible to chart precisely what happened to Jack and Diane. The protagonists and closest witnesses are no longer alive, and Carol was too young to remember. Like so many hasty wartime unions, the marriage proved to have no resistance to the less dramatic but more persistent pressures of peacetime — particularly, in the beginning, Jack's long absences in the hospital. Diane was probably much too young and volatile to handle life with a husband who was no longer the healthy, romantic young lieutenant but a thin, damaged veteran desperate to find his voice again. The stresses on both sides must have been considerable. What's more, after his rush into marriage with a girl he scarcely knew, by 1947 Jack was finding himself increasingly drawn to someone else.

John and Marshall Woodbridge, recorded by Esther as having brought Jack to the Langstaffs' 1945 Christmas carol party, were father and daughter, part of another musical family in the Brooklyn Heights circle. The senior Langstaffs and Woodbridges had been close friends since they were young. John's wife, Eleanor Woodbridge, known as Butsy, was a pianist who had made her debut at Town Hall in New York during the 1920s, but had (in those days of convention-impelled choice) given up the prospect of a concert career in order to have children. Later she did teach music, though, and David Langstaff was one of her piano pupils. Being also fond of his brothers, she had been writing Jack newsy, comforting letters all through his time in the Pacific. ("Another nice letter from Butsy," he wrote home. "She *is* a *dear!*")

Marshall was the elder Woodbridge daughter. Her younger sister was another attractive Eleanor, known as Nancy. Since her childhood Nancy had had little contact with Jack, having been away acquiring degrees first at Vassar and then the Cranbrook Academy of Art, in Michigan. But she and her mother were friends of Diane Guggenheim, now Langstaff, and Nancy was not only a painter but an excellent pianist. She also rode horses, at the Woodbridge house near the Guggenheim country home where Diane and her frail convalescent husband often stayed after Jack was finally released from the hospital, and she saw a great deal of them both.

"Diane would watch me getting the horse over the jumps, and I'd go back to their house," Nancy says. "I think Jack found that interesting, this person in jodhpurs smelling of horses."

She was not always in jodhpurs, though, and unlike Diane, she came from a family as intensely musical as Jack's. He was desperate now to get his voice back, and Butsy and her daughter were close at hand and willing to help. Diane was certainly musical, but she had always been what her daughter later described as "a needy person," and was no better equipped to accompany her singer husband at the piano than she was to nurse him back to health. There's no firsthand record of Diane's opinions, behavior, or emotions at this point, or even of where she may have been most of the time.

"Jack and I began to make music together," Nancy says. "I'd play for him to sing. My mother was a sort of coach, for me and for Jack, on musical aspects like phrasing — to this day I still see her little marks on things. It was wonderful for Jack because he wasn't ready for a professional coach. He was still recovering — still very skinny, maybe a hundred and twenty pounds."

In their 2005 book *The Guggenheims: A Family History,* Irwin and Debi Unger observe that "Diane's life was a restless quest for fulfilling experiences and relationships." Perhaps the restlessness took over early on, when it came to coping with baby Carol; Jack reported later that "Nancy took care of Carol a lot of the time when I was recuperating." He knew he was falling in love, and he tried to broach the subject to Nancy. She declined to listen, but it made no difference. One way or another, by early 1947 the brief Langstaff marriage was evaporating, by mutual consent.

In June 1947, with agreement from Diane, Jack went to Reno for a quick divorce, the petition claiming "extreme cruelty, mental in nature" as a necessary technicality. "I had to save money, so I shared a room with a crazy trumpeter," he said later. He also tried to raise money by giving a concert in Reno, with or without the trumpeter, but for an engagingly characteristic reason this didn't succeed. Meredith Langstaff wrote to Jack's Reno lawyer:

> I am very much amused at the odd turn in Jack's financial plans. Apparently he started to work up a concert to cover expenses when he heard that a three-year-old tot had fallen in one of the irrigation ditches and drowned; this being the third instance of the sort in the course of ten days, Jack felt that he should give the whole proceeds of the concert to the fund being raised to make the irrigation ditches safe against the meanderings of small children.
>
> I hope you find time to attend the concert.
> Cordially yours,
> B. Meredith Langstaff

On July 11 the lawyer cabled Meredith: "DECREE GRANTED EVERYTHING CONCLUDED SATISFACTORILY."

In 1948 Jack married Nancy Woodbridge. Their life together was full of music from the beginning. She accompanied him at two recitals that July, one a benefit for the Public Hall in Hamburg, Connecticut, and the other at Yale. In May, he'd sung in Handel's *Samson* at St. Thomas's, for the Oratorio Society of New York. From the time he came home from the war, it took his lungs two years to recover full capacity for singing, and he never did attempt the operatic roles he had set out for himself in that letter home in 1945. Instead he shifted his sights, in the general direction of recitals and oratorio.

Rather than go back to Curtis, he took voice lessons at the Juilliard School of music in New York; as a veteran, he had financial help through the GI Bill of Rights. "And I looked up my great lieder teacher, Leo Rosenek, and studied with him. Nancy used to come to some of my classes, sometimes she'd play Schumann and Hugo Wolf for me — she got lots from him as well." At Juilliard Jack was what Nancy diplomatically calls "an erratic student. . . . Studying was painful for Jack, he didn't like it — he loved learning, but not under a rigid routine." Outside the routine he was also taking lessons from his operatic Uncle Arthur once more, and he found these the most valuable of all.

Nancy used to go to these lessons too, as Jack's accompanist. She says Arthur Geary was a very little man with a large voice and a bad temper. "Jack could hardly get through a single phrase before Arthur would say something terrible, and sometimes I'd sit at the piano and cry with anger. There was Arthur telling him how badly he sang . . . but he was a very good voice teacher. He taught Jack how to breathe with his wounded lungs, he taught him tone, technique."

Then in 1949 Douglas Kennedy took a part in Jack's life again. As the longtime director of the English Folk Dance and Song Society, successor to Cecil Sharp, he was a prime force in England for keeping folk song from dropping into academic obscurity, and he invited Jack to come to London to make two records of English folk songs for the record label HMV. These were the early days of vinyl records, and HMV, christened His Master's Voice from its famous logo of a dog listening to an early gramophone horn, was part of the now-giant EMI Group.

"HMV had made recordings of bands playing folk songs," Jack said, "and Douglas suggested it would be wonderful to record some of the songs Cecil Sharp had collected."

Off went Jack to London, and Nancy with him. Meredith paid their way. They traveled in a freighter carrying iron ore, which was not the swiftest or easiest way to cross the Atlantic.

"We were the only passengers," Nancy says. "There was one tiny little stateroom on the ship, and the only exercise you could take was walking around the deck, which the captain didn't like. We ate with the sailors. And we used the sailors' bathroom, which had a curtain instead of a door, and Jack had to stand in front of the curtain when I went in."

Life wasn't much more luxurious when they reached London, which was still in the postwar austerity period that gripped Britain until 1951, with food and gasoline even more severely rationed than they had been during the war. They stayed in a boardinghouse. "And I remember Douglas Kennedy picking us up near Lord's Cricket Ground," Jack said, "and taking us to those great studios at Abbey Road." He recorded his folk songs; Nancy said later that she felt they were the best recordings he ever made. She accompanied him on some of them. "And in those days recording was all done on wax — if you made a mistake, you had to do the whole thing over again."

And the sound engineer was one George Martin, later to become famous and knighted for his accomplishments in the recording industry, not least the introduction of the Beatles. The lifelong friendships Jack made in England — particularly with George and Judy Martin, and later with Ralph and Ursula Vaughan Williams — had very deep roots.

Back in America, Jack gave his New York debut recital at Town Hall on Monday, November 14, 1949, "assisted by Felix Wolfes at the Piano." The *New York Times* critic reported that "a strong and sound musical instinct triumphed over an undependable vocal method."

His taste, intelligence, and feeling for music of various schools were fine enough to make him worth listening to, even if the way he produced his voice made for inconsistency of sound.

It is not often that one encounters a young singer with such a natural gift for music. Apparently he has also cultivated literature and languages. When he sang last night in German, Italian, and French, you had the feeling that he thoroughly understood the lines that precipitated the music. This is not a mean accomplishment; there are plenty of singers who sing as if they had not the faintest idea of what the words meant.

Mr. Langstaff's program, which covered quite a bit of territory as to schools and composers, was not sufficiently varied in quality. Much of it was slow, sad, and subdued. But because he is a good musician he managed to give it variety. Handel, Bach, Mozart, Gluck, Schubert, Wolf, Brahms, Duparc, Debussy, Mary Howe, Samuel Barber, Randall Thompson, Douglas Moore, Celius Dougherty, and old French and English songs were differentiated and grasped. Felix Wolfes helped with sensitive accompaniments.

Mr. Langstaff's voice is ample in size and pleasant in quality. But it is constricted in its upper range; it lacks breath support; it is not sufficiently colored or controlled. Since Mr. Langstaff is young, it is not too late to repair the damage. He has time to become an outstanding singer.

A year later, on November 13, 1950, he gave a second recital at Town Hall. A different critic for the *New York Times* was equally avuncular.

He has gone far toward overcoming the vocal deficiencies reported after his debut a year ago. The voice is limited in range but its extremes are no longer forced, except when he grew tired at the close of each half, and, although it has little natural resonance, it is liquid in quality and varied in color. And he used it with the easy eloquence of a folk singer.

Ballads in French, German, and English formed the substance of his program. The baritone sang Cantaloube's arrangements of folk songs from the Auvergne and another sweet group from ancient France with impeccable diction even when the melody bounced with high spirits. Lieder by Brahms and Schumann received the same unaffectedly artful treatment and so did some rather disingenuous songs by contemporary American and British composers.

James Quillian provided the piano accompaniments for Mr. Langstaff, who seemed to take as much joy in his music as he gave.

Of the "rather disingenuous" contemporary American songs, one was by Nancy's sister, Marshall, and one by Jeanne Behrend. Then, as later, he enjoyed showing off the work of friends — so long as it was good enough.

The critic for the *Herald Tribune* said of the 1950 recital:

Mr. Langstaff projects sentiment surely and maintains a mood firmly. As a musician, he seems to understand his own limitations, and he chose a program which leaned heavily on music of a folk nature. But there is no criticism here, for in all his numbers he gave his phrases wings, kept them moving and sprightly. Mr. Langstaff is not yet an assured technican. His range is rather limited and the size of his voice small. But he accomplished a remarkable amount with what technique he has already acquired. Mr. Langstaff really sings, and he makes music doing it.

There's a quality in these reviews that you find too in a 1950 comment by Edward Sackville-West in the *New Statesman and Nation,* in London; he's reviewing two of Jack's HMV recordings:

These records are wholly delightful and should on no account be missed. Mr. Langstaff is, it appears, an American: his voice is charming in quality, admirably controlled, and his diction is excellent. It is a long time since I heard folk songs delivered with so unemphatic an appreciation of their humor and pathos.

You can feel these critics struggling to point out some limitations (even Sackville-West, with his enigmatic "Mr. Langstaff is, it appears, an American"), but it's clear that he had captivated them. Even in the formal structure of recital or record, Jack was already accomplishing the thing he did best: making people enjoy music.

Until he was about thirty-five, he and Nancy lived in a third-floor walk-up in New York. ("At number 415 East 50th Street — we knew some people who owned a brownstone there, and we rented the top floor.") Brooklyn Heights and the family Christmas carols were in easy reach, just over the Brooklyn Bridge. Life was now a mix of music and babies: John was born in 1950, Gary in 1952, and Deborah in 1954. Living with three small children at the top of three flights of stairs, Nancy had her hands full, and she accompanied only the occasional local concert; Jack was away a lot of the time. He gave recitals all over the country, with assorted pianists.

The balance of his programs was still idiosyncratic, Nancy says. "He liked to begin with Handel, the big operatic songs. Then maybe Debussy. Singing in English mostly, because of his audience. And he'd end with a group of traditional songs, which no one else was doing then. He sang Britten, too — nobody else did, they were singing the French and the Germans. Jack searched out English composers, and Americans like Barber and Copland — though he never liked Copland much, those arranged folk songs weren't his favorites."

The work was varied, to say the least. Within a sample summer, he was giving a recital of Byrd and Dowland on a university campus; then a bunch of sea chanteys at the Waldorf-Astoria with the University Glee Club of New York City; then starring for a week in the musical *Anything Goes* in Worcester, Massachusetts; then teaching folk song at a summer school for the Country Dance Society of America. He had a manager now, Henry Colbert of Colbert-LaBerge Concert Management; he was a busy singer.

At one point in the mid-1950s, Henry Colbert sent him to see Leonard Bernstein, the wunderkind who was only two years older than Jack but already world famous as a conductor. "He's writing this show called *Candide*," said Colbert, "and I want you to sing for him."

So Jack went. "I was so naive," he said. "I got *Candide* mixed up with Shaw's *Candida*, so I thought I should sing something British, maybe Gilbert and Sullivan. I walked in and there was Bernstein, and he said, 'What will you sing?' And I said, 'The ghost song from

Ruddigore.' And do you know, he just sat down at the piano and played it, right off."

And Bernstein hired Jack to play Candide for the backers' audition, a single performance for the show's potential investors — but that was all.

So the round of recitals and concerts went on. Jack sang for Young People's Concerts at Constitution Hall with the National Symphony Orchestra, and at Carnegie Hall with the New York Philharmonic. He sang medieval music for the annual Garden Party for the members of the Metropolitan Museum of Art. He toured. He went several times to Britain, to give recitals or to record folk songs. But he wasn't making a great deal of money.

Carol Preston, the teacher who had revealed the world of folk song and folk dance to Jack when he was fifteen, had moved in 1938 to Washington, D.C., after being appointed headmistress of the Potomac School. With her went her friend Helen Seth-Smith, as associate headmistress — and there they stayed, for the next twenty-three years. Carol had remained a close friend of the Langstaff family, and she and Helen had a cottage out in the country, which Jack and Ken had visited.

Another old friend remembers being invited there to a weekend party with them — and remembers too the effect Jack had on her, which was shared by numbers of spellbound ladies in the course of his long life. "It was a glorious weekend," she says, "nonstop wonderful, with Jack singing folk songs, and sword dancing. He was the man of my dreams. But he was twenty-six and engaged to be married, and I was seventeen years old. So he married Nancy, and I went to university."

Now, in 1955, Carol Preston came up with her second beneficent effect on Jack's future. He and Nancy had just had their third baby, Deborah. The Potomac School had moved out of the city to a large new campus in McLean, Virginia, and Carol had been asking Jack to give her the names of people who might come to run the school's music program. Finally she asked if he would come and do it himself.

Jack protested that he wasn't a teacher, and at first he refused. But Carol persisted — this was, after all, the woman who had pulled him out of the coat closet in grade school — and eventually Jack agreed. As they both knew very well, now that he had a wife and three small children to support, he needed a day job. The school would pay him a regular salary, Nancy would also teach there, and their children could attend the school. And Carol promised that he would be allowed to continue his career as a singer at the same time.

"He never got to the point where he could support himself solely by singing," Nancy says. "You have to be at the very top to do that. I think he hoped he would, at the beginning, but it didn't happen — partly because what was appreciated at that time was a much more operatic kind of voice. Jack had a more personal voice; it wasn't what the public expected. He wanted to sing lieder; he was drawn to the so-called art songs rather than opera — though he did like to do oratorio in churches, like *Elijah*.

"So we went to Potomac."

CHAPTER SEVEN

"Mr. Langstaff could make an onion sing!"

*T*he Potomac School had opened in 1904, with 48 students, on Dupont Circle in Washington, D.C. It was a day school, and since its move four years earlier to the 55-acre campus in McLean, Virginia, it now had more than 400 students, from kindergarten to grade 8. Initially, grades 1–3 were coeducational; grades 4–8 were girls. Nancy taught the lower grades, and Jack taught the girls to sing.

"His teaching was not traditional, and he didn't have a good sense of how to control a class," Nancy says. "He'd yell at them, very loudly. But once he got into teaching them the songs, they were absolutely with him."

Jack's infectious enthusiasm filled the Potomac School with music, peaking around Christmas and May Day. Neither he nor Carol Preston had much time for institutional music, like School

Songs, and he was never even required to teach his students "The Star-Spangled Banner." Instead he brought music alive through performance, often involving the entire school population — as in 1958, when they gave one of the first U.S. performances of Benjamin Britten's *Noye's Fludde.*

Britten, whose work Jack had always admired, had often written wonderful things for young voices. He was also often at odds with the English musical establishment, but it was the senior English composer Ralph Vaughan Williams, always benign, who told Jack in 1958 about *Noye's Fludde.* Britten had written this enchanting opera almost entirely for children, basing it on a mystery play from the fifteenth-century Chester Cycle, and had presented it for the first time that summer at his Aldeburgh Festival in Suffolk, in the Orford Parish Church. The only adult parts were Noye, Mrs. Noye, and the Voice of God, and much of the orchestral accompaniment was written deliberately simply for strings, recorders, bugles, handbells, and assorted percussion, including homemade instruments, like sandpaper blocks. Britten specified that the opera should always be performed in a church or a hall, not in a theater; that the congregation (he avoided the word "audience") should not applaud; and that they should sing the three hymns he included in the score.

Jack of course loved this last element, particularly the use of the hymn "Eternal Father" to calm the storm of the Great Flood. He brought the score of *Noye's Fludde* home from Britain, and he plunged the whole Potomac community into making an opera, under his direction. He also sang Noye, looking suitably senior in the square, rather Amish-looking beard he sometimes grew in the Fifties. The production was so successful that some years later they did it again, with children from three other schools, at the National Cathedral in Washington, D.C. "Potomac did wonderful costumes, they really got into it," Nancy says. "He had the entire school singing, and strings, recorders, two pianos — I played, with another teacher. After that he did the *Play of Daniel* too."

Jack taught at Potomac for twelve years. His own children were among his students — including the teenage Carol, for a while. "By then," says Deborah Langstaff, "he was very strict — if someone was chewing gum, he'd make them swallow it. But as a father, if he found you reading under the covers with a flashlight, and you looked up at him with your finger on your lips, he could be counted on not to say a word."

Though he was often away, Jack's impact on the Potomac community was so striking that long after he left, when Potomac had grown to a K–12 coeducational school of 950 pupils, they named their splendid new assembly hall the Langstaff Auditorium. Decades later, when the Revels was an established institution and he was traveling to some new city hoping to set up its own productions, he would first seek out any former Potomac students living in the area. He knew they would be natural supporters, and of course they always were.

One nameless student tried to record his extraordinary effect on them all in a little Potomac School newsletter called *The Elephant's Trunk,* mourning Jack's departure at the end of his time as music director.

When the students that have been going to Potomac for the past twelve years or so become middle-aged, and music is a part of their lives, they will understand why. It was Mr. Langstaff.

When we were in the lower school, we were taught by Mr. Langstaff to sing "Christ*mass*," and it has stuck with us ever since. Everyone at Potomac sings "Christ*mass*" and they will always sing it that way. We do not realize how unique it is because it is a part of us, much the way singing old English pub songs through the school halls is. It was Mr. Langstaff.

At Potomac there is a singing atmosphere. Every morning the upper school sings a song in assembly. Every Monday, most of the school does so together. At Christmas, everyone takes part in a singing program. The whole school turns itself to music. It was Mr. Langstaff. All of the students, indeed, all of the people who ever knew Mr. Langstaff were infected with his dynamic enthusiasm for music, which he loves, because it is his life. Because Mr. Langstaff loves it with such energy, he taught it well. He loves children, and is a great teacher. His enthusiasm for music has passed on to the students, to stay with them the rest of their lives, and inadvertently, through their love of music, passed on to the parents. Everyone associated with Potomac has a passion for music. It was Mr. Langstaff.

Mr. Langstaff could make people produce. He could make the smallest child or the biggest adult sing, and love it. Mr. Langstaff could make an onion sing!

Mr. Langstaff's leaving is not just the going away of a teacher. It is the going away of a life at Potomac, leaving a great gap in the school. There will be other music teachers, other Christmas plays, other music classes, other *Noye's Fluddes,* but not another Mr. Langstaff.

Even after Jack died, more than forty years later, there was an outpouring of affectionate reminiscence from his former Potomac pupils, now indeed well into middle age.

"He would always get us to sing loudly, and stand up to sing," one of them wrote. "He told us, 'If you're going to make a mistake, don't shrink down and try to hide it' (he bent over to demonstrate, with a little pained, fearful look on his face). 'Stand up' (he rose up super tall) 'and make a BIG mistake!' I've followed that advice ever since, and it's saved me a lot of time and hedging in many situations."

They had never forgotten him. "I remember him, during music classes in the old field house," wrote another, "stomping passionately around the room, throwing his entire body into the music in an effort to get us to sing louder and with more gusto. He simply would not tolerate wimpy singing. Also, we all had to start singing right on the first note of the song (what he called the attack) or he would make us start over and over until we got it right."

It was summed up best, perhaps, by a former student named Ann Bradley Vehslage:

I graduated from Potomac with the ninth-grade class of 1955, and was fortunate to have special time with Mr. Langstaff as he taught me the songs I would sing as Ariel in that year's ninth-grade play, Shakespeare's The Tempest.

Many of us had a crush on Mr. Langstaff. His huge, joyous, creative talent, his enthusiasm for teaching us the wonderful and original holiday songs he selected each year, and, of course, his striking good looks made for wonderful times at Potomac. I cherish those memories to this day.

Each year in the Christmas play, we would sing our little hearts out as he directed us with a big smile on his face, urging us to do our best. And, thanks to Mr. Langstaff, I know now that we really were quite good! My mother later told me there were few dry eyes in the house when we sang, and although we were unaware of this, we all certainly knew we were having a ball. We were being taught by a master, and were truly privileged to be his students. I will remember him always, with affection and admiration.

By nature, Jack was not so much a teacher as a missionary. It was his passion for communicating the joy of music that entranced these children, and for that matter anyone of any age who ever sang or worked with him. He was a firm believer in the principle of "learn it by doing it" and always maintained that music education was a matter of collaboration as much as instruction.

He had already begun working with children on radio and television. The first connection had come in 1949, after he had made his two English records of folk songs for HMV at the Abbey Road Studios. Before he left, he had asked HMV if they would consider his doing some songs with children.

I said, I've got some from the Just So Stories, or Winnie-the-Pooh. . . ."Oh, no," they said, "not that nanny stuff." "Well, then," I said, "folk songs." So we ended up recording a lot of those. All the records were 12-inch 78s in those days, two songs per side — you made about half a cent per song. I had a blind pianist accompanying me, Sam Mason. He would read Cecil Sharp's tunes in braille, and sometimes he'd improvise. He was wonderful.

Through the good offices of Douglas Kennedy, at some recording sessions Jack was also accompanied at the piano by the legendary Gerald Moore — who later played for his London debut recital at the Wigmore Hall. ("A singer whose verbal and musical intelligence is well out of the ordinary," said the London *Times*.) And it was through Kennedy that Jack had become a friend of Ralph Vaughan Williams and other major figures on the musical scene.

Everybody knew everybody in that English music world — Douglas was married to Helen Karpeles, who was the sister of Maud Karpeles, who was close to Ursula Wood, who lived with the Vaughan Williamses and of course was later Lady Vaughan Williams . . . so Douglas took me down to Dorking to meet VW in 1949. He was a very sweet guy. Later, one summer when I was over doing recordings, I stayed there with them, and Percy Grainger came by. . . . And VW came to my debut recital at the Wigmore Hall, I remember — and turned his hearing aid off when I sang a song by Charles Ives.

Besides the network of celebrated friends, this small world also included every music producer at the British Broadcasting Corporation. Before long, Jack's visits to England in the fifties were devoted not only to making recordings but also to singing with children on programs for the celebrated Schools division of BBC Radio. In classrooms all over Britain, by all accounts he had even the most resistant pupils singing along with him for twenty minutes three times a week. In due course BBC Television discovered him as well, and he made four seasons of a program called *Making Music,* coaxing a group of children in a television studio — and those on the other side of the television screen — into singing and playing simple instruments. Everyone had a very good time, even the cameramen, and the programs were later broadcast to schools in Canada and Australia. The deputy head of BBC Schools Television described the series as "one of the jewels in the crown of early Schools Television, which helped to revolutionize primary school music teaching."

Jack was still making records for HMV, overseen by George Martin at the Abbey Road Studios. Altogether he recorded about eighty-five folk songs, sometimes departing from the convention of piano accompaniment and singing to a guitar, or *a cappella*. Many were what we would call children's songs ("Dance to Your Daddy" . . ."What'll We Do with the Baby?") but were not at first marketed as such.

Then about that time we made an LP for children with some wonderful folk songs that had never been recorded before, and I included some things we'd done for the BBC programs. They were orchestrated by Ron Goodwin, a friend of George Martin's, and I conducted them with a small orchestra of children playing instruments. We called it Songs for Singing Children.

Songs for Singing Children was one of his most successful recordings, and was followed by another, *Let's Make Music*. Like the first, it had notes by John Hosier, Jack's *Making Music* producer and the BBC's greatest champion of music for children. Jack's professional life was always full of cross-fertilization. In the recording studio, as on television, he led choruses of English schoolchildren in folk songs and singing games. To his mind, that was always the best way of making records for children. "All my work with children is about participation — I'm not just interested in singing *for* children. Even with solo songs, I hope they'll join in."

Soon he was reaching children not just through records but through books. Jack became a published author almost by accident, in the leaner years before he went to Potomac or made his BBC TV series. As a present for their small son John, he and Nancy — who was still an artist as well as a musician — had made a little book from "Frog Went A-Courtin'," one of Jack's favorite folk songs. He had compiled the words from several British and American variants, and used the tune he remembered from his own childhood. "And Nancy did two drawings for it," he said, "one brownish, one greenish."

One day in 1954 this book was lying on the table of their apartment in New York when Esther and Meredith Langstaff came to tea, bringing a friend of theirs named Louise Seaman Bechtel, who edited the children's book reviews in the *New York Herald Tribune.* Ms. Bechtel picked up the book — or considering the family history, perhaps Esther picked it up and handed it to her. Jack was astonished by her reaction.

Miss Bechtel looked at the book and said, "You should take this to a publisher." Well, I didn't even know there were such things as children's book publishers. So she gave us a list of ten children's book editors, all women, with the youngest at the top of the list — and that was Margaret K. McElderry at Harcourt, Brace, so I went and showed it to her.

Margaret McElderry had a nature as full of enthusiasms as Jack's, but she also had a strong business sense. She told Jack that *Frog Went A-Courtin'* would make an excellent picture book, but that since Nancy was probably not familiar with the four-color separation process necessary in those days, the pictures should be done by a professional illustrator, perhaps her friend Fritz Eichenberg.

"So I walked out," Jack said.

But I was only doing a few concerts then, trying to make a living, and when I went home and told Nancy, she said, "Look, if Margaret would like to do the book, let her. I don't care about the drawings — we need the money." So I went back to Margaret and explained, and she was very nice, and she said maybe Fritz Eichenberg wouldn't do it but there was this famous artist from Europe who'd done some books for Golden Press, The Three Bears *and a* Mother Goose, *and his contract was coming up for renewal and maybe she could get him. That was Feodor Rojankovsky, and she did get him, and he did the book and it won the Caldecott Medal.*

According to Margaret McElderry, the Caldecott and Newbery Medals did more to increase a book's sales than a Pulitzer Prize.

So Margaret calls me up and says, "Quick, we need another book that Feodor Rojankovsky can do." And I looked at "Over in the Meadow" in Cecil Sharp's folk-song collection — he'd taken it out later because it wasn't really a folk song, the words had come from a poem by a woman in the nineteenth century. I made up some words, with help from Deborah, who was two or three years old at the time — and that was my next book with Rojankovsky.

It was a beautiful book, even more engaging than the first. By the end of his life, Jack had published more than thirty books, many of them — like the glowing first two — picture books based on annotated folk songs. One of them is his version of the folk play *St. George and the Dragon,* drawn from several of the oldest English texts; it became the basis for every variant of the play that's been performed in the Christmas Revels from the beginning. Writing was not his favorite occupation, and Nancy acted as his first editor and sometimes collaborator, but the impetus always came from Jack; his enthusiasm shines out of all the books.

In 1966 Jack was persuaded by Lavinia Russ—another feisty book person, a senior version of Margaret McElderry—to take books to children, and parents, through television. American TV had already learned from the BBC about his talent for teaching music through performance, and he had done a series of programs of songs with children on WNDT-TV in New York. This new book series was to be called *Children Explore Books*; he enjoyed it, he said.

Lavinia had convinced NBC Television to do a weekly program on children's books, so for a while I led this double life, teaching at Potomac in the week and flying to New York on Friday night to have a script conference at NBC. We'd rehearse on Saturday morning—they'd picked children of all ages—and then we'd come on set and tape for two hours on Saturday afternoon. I was the moderator. We'd have a theme—say it was pirates—and I'd get them talking, to and fro, all on camera, in a room full of books, and I'd have an old flintlock or a pirate song. Then Lavinia would have a new book, and I could read some of it to them—then they'd come back the next week having read it themselves, and we'd discuss it. We did twenty-six programs all told.

"Double life" was an understatement as a description of his time at Potomac. Here's a "Studio Note" from the magazine *Musical Courier* written late in 1957. Bear in mind that it deals with a man also employed as music director of a notable school.

John Langstaff is now on an extensive tour that will take him across the country to Texas, Colorado, up the West Coast to Yakima, Washington, and into the key cities of British Columbia. After Trans-Canada broadcasts and recitals in

Vancouver, the baritone swings back to New York City for the Town Hall Christmas concert, followed by a Christmas recital production in Washington, D.C. In the late winter, this busy artist . . . sings the Bach Kreuzstab Cantata with the Saidenburg Symphony in New York; is soloist with the Springfield, Massachusetts, Symphony in February; is booked for the world premiere of Antal Dorati's work for baritone and orchestra in Minneapolis and an all-French recital in Washington, D.C.

So it went on, for the next ten years. From his family base in McLean, Virginia, Jack sang in a total of forty-seven of the states of the Union, including a twenty-eight-concert tour of Alaska; he had joined the roster of the Eastman Boomer concert management. *Glamour* magazine published a picture of him that was indeed glamorous, and said felicitously that he had "a voice like strong, dark honey."

Always his concerts included his trademark mix of the classic and the modern. Among the American composers whose work he sang, Jack's closest friend was John Edmunds, who was some years older — he had been a contemporary of Jeanne Behrend's at Curtis — but was very much like him in enthusiasm, creativity, and perhaps temperament. Edmunds was a scholar of early music: medieval, Renaissance, and baroque music, from the Middle Ages to about the time of Mozart. His own work included beautiful settings of poems ranging from Middle English texts to Yeats and Hardy. The two of them fizzed with ideas for joint projects, though they were seldom both in the same place at the same time. Edmunds wrote in 1959:

There is no one alive, dear Jack, with whom I'd rather work in presenting recitals of my own songs, and my editions of

Purcell, Scarlatti, the German and French folk songs, etc., etc.,
than you. I hope that we can find a means of bringing this
about someday.

Eventually they did play concerts together, starting with one at
Carnegie Recital Hall in November 1960, and in 1966 Jack flew out
to California to take part in a major concert of Edmunds's work, at
Berkeley. "You are the most profoundly interesting and thorough-
going artist I've ever worked with," Edmunds wrote to Jack, and the
admiration was mutual. Jack said, decades later:

He was wonderful, such an interesting man. We did things of
Scarlatti's that he'd found in libraries in Italy, that nobody had
ever heard. He had a way of playing the piano like Benjamin
Britten — strong hands, a lot of energy. And his mind darted
about. . . . Once we were doing a big white-tie concert in
Washington, D.C., and we went out on the stage, and John
walked right past me and out again. I thought wildly that
maybe my fly was open, so I dropped my hands . . . but he
came back and sat down at the piano and off we went. He'd
forgotten his music — left it at the hotel.

They could both be a little scattered at times, though the music
would never suffer. Jack was devoted to John Edmunds, and cham-
pioned his work for the rest of his life. One of the most enduring
things they had in common was an instinct for combining the
power of words with the power of music; for a summer session at
the Potomac School in 1965, Edmunds provided Jack with a musical
score to which the students were to set their own narrative.

Jack took this one stage further by intermixing poetry and
music in a program called *Voyages,* which he took on the road for

several seasons in the 1960s with the actress-singer Robin Howard and the folk musician Happy Traum. In an interview in 1989 he said that he got the idea for this in Europe, from seeing a program of readings and songs done by Robert Graves and the Scottish singer Isla Cameron. "It's interesting that in a way, that was the seed of the Revels idea: to gather songs and stories on one theme and put them together."

At Potomac, his wife pinch-hit for him if he was away singing. "I covered his classes for him when he was on tour, and they gave me a hard time," Nancy says. "They wanted this glamorous fellow, and they got this . . . *woman*."

And in the end, the school lost its beloved music director entirely. He was simply too busy, especially in Britain. The *Making Music* TV series was in full swing, and he was crossing the Atlantic every year, to give concerts or to record, or both. He was, temporarily, a sort of honorary Brit, to the point that when the English Folk Dance and Song Society held its 1958 Diamond Jubilee celebration in London, the singer was not a native-born Englishman but Jack Langstaff. (Ralph Vaughan Williams cut the birthday cake — and was in the audience when Jack, singing the ballad "Sir Patrick Spens," had a sudden terrible memory lapse. He mouthed to Isla Cameron, who was sitting in the front row, *What's next?* And she mouthed back the next line, and on Jack went. History doesn't record whether Vaughan Williams noticed.)

Finally Jack was doing so much for the BBC, and had so many friends and colleagues in Britain, that in 1967 he left the Potomac School and took the entire family to London for a year. The only one left behind was John, who was in boarding school.

But by the time he left, Jack would have had two dry runs for his Christmas Revels.

CHAPTER EIGHT

"I LOST MY SHIRT."

*J*ack's fascination with the world of folk song and dance hadn't waned since the adolescent years when he learned to dance the Morris and heard English folk music sung by Appalachian descendants of the settlers who had brought it with them. By the time he was in his thirties he was a major presence at Pinewoods, the camp on Long Pond, Massachusetts, at which the then Country Dance Society of New York ran summer programs, and in 1951 he founded and ran a Folk Music Week there to stress the element of song. This took persistence: after a couple of years the singers had to share their week with dance, and then with recorder playing, but by 1962 Jack and Frank Warner were directing a full Folk Music Week again.

For the Langstaff children, John, Gary, and Deborah, Pinewoods was an idyllic summer home all through the years when both their parents were teaching at Potomac. They roamed the camp's twenty-five acres of woodland, they swam in Long Pond, which is the size of a small lake. And above all, says Deborah, now a singer herself, they were all together, dancing and making music with other families whose names have resonance now in the folk world: the Ritchies, the Warners, the Chapins.

Every summer we went for a whole month, always in the same house on the shore of the lake, all taking part in the music and dance with the grown-ups. It was an incredible togetherness — and formative for me, that's for sure.

Jerry Epstein, Jack's friend and often accompanist, remembers the impact of hearing him sing at Pinewoods in 1966:

Jack was singing "All Around My Hat"— I remember it as if it were yesterday. I was looking at the people in the room, coming from the pressure and hassle of New York or Boston or wherever and shedding all of that baggage of civilization, listening to Jack weave his magic. The saying that would not leave my head was "To enter the Kingdom of Heaven you must become as a little child." It seemed to me that I saw that happening all around me to people who were quite unaware of it.

The small dedicated world of folk song and folk dance is full of joyous enthusiasts; it's no wonder Jack felt at home in it. Many folk songs are melancholy, for sure; many are about death and desolation, and some are positively ghoulish. But people who sing and dance together tend to be upbeat by nature and to have a strong sense of community. If the first seed of Jack's vision of a Christmas Revels came from the family carol parties of his boyhood, the second must have come in the 1950s from the Christmas Country Ball of the Country Dance Society of America. This was a cheery annual event held a week or two before Christmas in New York City, at Hunter College on Union Square West. It was directed by May Gadd, with Philip Merrill conducting, and it was basically a Christmas dance party — but within it were at least three elements, all inherited from English tradition, which would become mainstays of Jack's Revels.

In intervals of the communal dancing at this party, there was a Mummers Play, ending with a Morris sword dance, both of which have roots in England's misty medieval past. There was the "Sussex Mummers' Carol," not quite so old; sung by local carolers called Tipteers, it was first written down in Sussex in 1880 and arranged by the composer Percy Grainger (whom Jack had first met in England, and who, like Vaughan Williams, loved to work with folk song). And there was the "Boar's Head Carol," sung by Jack at the party while the wassail bowl and a fake boar's head were ceremonially carried in. This tradition is certainly old; there were as many wild pigs in early Britain as there are deer in modern New England, and the serving of a boar's head on festive occasions goes back to Roman Britain. The carol dates from the sixteenth century, and to this day it's still sung in a Christmas procession at Queen's College, Oxford, as chefs march into the dining hall bearing a platter with the roasted head of a real pig holding an apple in its mouth. As for the wassail bowl, it dates back to the Middle Ages and even to the Vikings; *wes hal* was an Old English greeting, "Be in good health," that evolved into a toast in the centuries after England was invaded by thirsty Danes.

On went the dancing, at the Country Dance Society's party, until everyone went home exhausted and happy at midnight. It must have been like a dance-focused version of the Langstaff family carol party, just as joyous, just as unforgettable. And its mixture of folk dance, folk song, and the spoken word stayed in Jack's mind and fermented. In 1957, two years after he began teaching at Potomac, he wove the three major elements into a more complicated pattern and took it public.

In the *New Yorker* magazine for December 14, 1957, downpage from listings for the current big musical hits (*My Fair Lady, West Side Story, Bells Are Ringing*) there is a very small advertisement:

CHRISTMAS MASQUE
of TRADITIONAL REVELS
FOR CHILDREN
MUSIC * DRAMA * DANCE
JOHN LANGSTAFF
Baritone Soloist with Audience Participation
N.Y.: TOWN HALL   DEC 29th at 3pm
D.C.: LISNER AUDITORIUM   Jan 4

"It came out of so many things," Jack said about thirty years ago, looking back. "The carols, and the folklore I'd taught to children . . . knowing Carol Preston, and May Gadd . . . having played St. George once when I was young . . . and wanting to relate things with early roots to modern forms of art, through Mary Craighill and the young dance company she had in Washington. . . . I thought I could dovetail all those things, which was what always interested me when I was building my own programs."

For the first time now, he was building not just a program, but a theatrical performance that was also a community event. It would be a great big public carol party, with Jack as the master of ceremonies, just as his father, Meredith, had presided over the Brooklyn Heights Christmas family gathering. The party would be held twice, in two ambitiously large spaces, each seating about 1,500 people: first at New York's Town Hall, on West 43rd Street, and six days later at Lisner Auditorium at George Washington University, D.C. Jack made the advance payments for the theater rentals out of his own not very deep pocket, and he had the Colbert agency, who booked his own concerts, as managers.

The program itself was full of his memories and his friends. From his days as a choirboy he had loved the sound of trumpets soaring above massed voices, so he hired the New York Brass Quintet. "We had them up in the audience for the carols — it was very exciting." Through teacher friends he acquired some singing children from the progressive City and Country School, in Greenwich Village. From Washington, D.C., where after two years at Potomac he now had nearly as many friends as in New York, he brought an experimental dance group recently formed by the dancer Mary Craighill, and he enlisted the Morris team he knew so well from Pinewoods summers. History doesn't record whether all these people had time for more than one rehearsal, but it probably didn't matter; the glue that held them all together was the voice, presence, and personality of their singer-director.

At the single New York performance, he came onstage and spoke to the audience, welcoming them, charming them, and telling them what to expect. Then after a rousing introduction from the brass quintet, the Morris men danced, in half-light, the Abbots Bromley Horn Dance, each of them holding a full set of antlers to his head. (This had, and has, an eerie quality in Revels, though in its English village of origin, where it still survives, a line of Morris men and traditional figures dance outdoors to a set of jaunty tunes all day long.) Then up came the lights and back came Jack, to lead the audience in "Deck the Hall with Boughs of Holly." And for the rest of the evening, performance and communal singing alternated.

The Morris men danced the stick-clashing "Brighton Camp," and everybody sang "Silent Night." Mary Craighill's Washington Contemporary Dance Group danced as Jack sang "The Cherry Tree Carol," and everybody sang "The Twelve Days of Christmas." Jack and the Craighill company performed "King Herod and the Cock," everybody sang "The First Nowell"; children processed in to sing and mime *I Saw Three Ships On Chris-i-mas Day in the Morning*, with its haunting, rising refrain, and everybody sang "O Come, All Ye Faithful." The Morris men "and some resting actors from off Broadway" performed the traditional death-and-revival Mummers' Play, with the sword dance from Ampleforth ending in its impressive star-shaped sword lock, and as a finale everybody sang the "Sussex Mummers' Carol."

"And I lost my shirt," Jack said.

The New York audience had had a very good time, but it wasn't large enough to cover the cost of renting Town Hall. "And since my concert manager managed it all, that was a cost. And although we had a very beautiful flyer, of a hobbyhorse, by my friend Ronnie Silbert, we didn't have any money for advertising — even though we had a great volunteer committee behind us."

The committee consisted of twenty-five ladies, and included not only his own mother but Diane's — and Betty Chapin, wife of Schuyler Chapin, later general manager of the Metropolitan Opera, whose son Hank would one day become a stalwart Revels player of the Fool in several cities, for years. At this point, however, Hank was only six years old. Carol Langstaff was about fourteen, helping backstage.

Six days later Jack did the same thing all over again in the Lisner Auditorium in D.C. "On the tenth day of Christmas," reported the *Washington Post* merrily, "John Langstaff gave to Washington a Christmas Masque."

Jack said, "The people from the Potomac School had said, 'Bring it down here and we'll get you an audience of fifteen hundred.' And they did, it sold out—but we'd brought the Morris dancers and the actors from New York, so we made a profit of about fifteen dollars. So for financial reasons, we decided not to do it again."

But nine years later, before Jack left Potomac, Fate presented him with a second dry run for the Revels. In 1966, NBC Television, for whom Jack had done his book series, deputed the director Isaiah Sheffer to find a Christmas special, and Sheffer (who later founded and ran Symphony Space, which became the home of the New York Revels) went to Jack. And Jack gave them the script and music from the Christmas Masque with which he had lost his shirt at the New York Town Hall in 1957.

I did stand onstage and talk to the audience, in those early performances at Town Hall and Lisner, so there was a kind of script. And NBC decided to do it. We used some of the same people—the brass, and Mary Craighill's dancers from Washington—and again we had some young unknown actors from New York. One of them was Dustin Hoffman, he was the Dragon in the Mummers' Play. He extemporized too much but he was very funny. . . . Seymour Barrett, who works on my books with me, he orchestrated the songs. There was a big studio with a set like Elizabethan England—snow all over the place, and lovely little lanterns. I hadn't been expecting that, but when I went into my dressing room there was this Elizabethan costume."

Perhaps they put him in those puffy knickers, with tights. He wore it all, anyway, and as before, he sang "The Cherry Tree Carol" for the dancers. And his first daughter, Carol, now twenty-three, sang the Hebridean "Christ Child's Lullaby." Isaiah Sheffer directed.

We rehearsed in the morning and recorded it in the afternoon. It was done in color, and shown on Christmas night. It was beautiful. And they erased it, alas.

But an audiotape of the televised Christmas Masque survives. Jack sings wonderfully, but sounds a little uneasy when he has to talk. As the Dragon, Dustin Hoffman uses a big deep voice and snarls a lot. (At this point in his life, Hoffman was playing jazz piano as much as acting, but a few months later Mike Nichols cast him in *The Graduate* and the balance shifted.)

The following year, off the Langstaffs went to spend their year in Britain. While they were there, an emissary came over from the Shady Hill School, a progressive K–8 private school in Cambridge, Massachusetts, to invite Jack to become its music director. His success at Potomac had given him a glowing reputation in the world of music education, and Shady Hill wanted to capture him before anyone else did.

By this point, as singer, teacher, or author, Jack had visited almost every major American city with an active interest in the arts, and the Cambridge/Boston area must have seemed a good fit. After the postwar recovery decade of the fifties, every kind of artistic endeavor was beginning to ferment in the sixties, in the United States as in Europe: theater, music, dance, painting, you name it. But the bubbles weren't yet visible everywhere. As an arts-obsessed young English journalist, I was sent by my London newspaper to the United States for four months in 1962, and I went home to report rather loftily that the only two places in which a civilized European could happily live seemed to me to be Cambridge, Massachusetts, and San Francisco, California. Maybe the Langstaffs agreed.

"I went to teach at Shady Hill in 1967," Jack said, "after swearing that I'd never teach again — at least not that age group."

Nancy says that they were attracted to the Cambridge area by the fact that their teenage children would now be close to urban amenities, rather than being relatively isolated in McLean, Virginia. (By now John was nineteen, Gary seventeen, and Deborah twelve.) They chose to live in Lexington, a suburban town renowned for its school system, and bought an enchanting eighteenth-century farmhouse with small rooms, low ceilings, and a garden in which Jack grew Concord grapes and took up beekeeping. Before long Nancy too began to teach again, at the Cambridge Friends School, which had been founded in 1961 as the only Quaker school in Massachusetts.

So, having moved to New England, Jack put down new roots, particularly in the world of the arts. For six years he bounced through life in much the same pattern as he had followed at Potomac: teaching, singing at recitals and concerts, touring, recording, turning folk songs into children's books, and encouraging audiences to sing in new productions of *Noye's Fludde* and similar family-oriented operas.

But at the back of his mind, the vision of a Revels was still simmering. He was entering his fifties now; for more than forty years his life had been twining together the strands spun by his interests and history. The joyous traditional celebration of Christmas; the liturgical splendor of the Anglican Church; the layered, myth-rooted simplicity of folk song and folk dance; the power of music in the teaching of children; the instinctive theatricality of a professional performer — all these were heaped up in the imagination of a musician who found his greatest delight in making audiences not just listen but sing.

The whole thing was like a bonfire waiting to be set alight, and around 1970 the spark was struck by a visit from the small daughter who had haunted his letters home from war when he was twenty-three. He had dedicated his first book, *Frog Went A-Courtin'*, to her, decades later: "For my Carol," the dedication read, "who was the first to give me the fun of singing with children." Now Carol was twenty-seven, having grown up to become a dancer-singer with an eclectic, very Langstaff mix of talents and tastes: early music, folk song, folk dance, modern dance. She came to visit one day devastated by a professional setback in New York, and Jack, trying to fill the gap, suggested that she help him develop a reincarnation of the Christmas Masque he had done in New York when she was fourteen.

And everything changed.

CHAPTER NINE

THE FIRST REAL REVELS

*C*arol Langstaff had had a fragmented childhood, spending part of each year with Jack and Nancy ("At first, I slept on two chairs pushed together in their cute New York apartment") and part with her mother, Diane. Her two worlds must have had wild discrepancies, but they were both full of music.

After her divorce from Jack, Diane was married for a few years to Robert Guillard, a marine biologist and musician whom she met through the Country Dance and Song Society. Already fascinated by folk song and folk dance, she then moved to Greenwich Village, where the folk revival scene was bubbling away in the 1950s and 1960s. After meeting the expatriate Irish singers Paddy and Tom Clancy she went to Ireland, comfortably funded by family money, to record folk songs from their family and others, and she was entranced by the youngest Clancy, Liam. They traveled together throughout Ireland, recording songs, and Diane brought him back to New York, where in 1956 she founded a company called Tradition Records. Paddy Clancy ran it for her, and they issued about forty-five records, not only by the Clancy Brothers and Tommy Makem but by a range of major figures from the thriving folk scene, including Odetta, Ewan MacColl, and John Jacob Niles.

The Langstaff divorce had truly been an amicable one. One of the first Tradition albums was a record entitled *JOHN LANGSTAFF Sings American and English Folk Songs and Ballads,* with Nancy Woodbridge at the piano.

After the Clancys signed with Columbia in 1961, Tradition faded and was sold to Everest Records, but Diane went on collecting folk songs in Ireland and Appalachia. She had learned to play the dulcimer, and sometimes sang and recorded herself as well. In 1963 she married William Meek, who wrote about folk music for the *Irish Times,* and thereafter lived mostly in Ireland, where they had two sons and adopted two daughters. She had begun calling herself Diane Hamilton, after a character in folk song named Mary Hamilton, and when ten years later she divorced William Meek and married her fourth husband, John Darby Stolt, Mr. Stolt obligingly changed his name to J.D. Hamilton.

Carol's times with her mother thus often became song-collecting trips, across the southwest of the U.S. or to Ireland — a country that she too found bewitching, so that the unconventional dance company that she eventually founded and now directs, Flock Dance Troupe, exists both in Vermont and in Galway. After leaving the Potomac School, Carol studied for a year or two at the Longy School of Music, in Cambridge, sometimes acting at Harvard's Loeb Drama Center and singing at the coffeehouse Club 47, later called Passim. In her teens she had found herself forming a warm relationship with her formidable grandfather Harry Guggenheim, who had had little interest in her when she was a small child. He took her to his favorite race meetings at Saratoga, and she stayed with him often at the family mansion Falaise, on Long Island; he told her she was too skinny, gave her money to buy warm clothes, and paid her medical bills.

But Carol, who had grown up with song and dance, and at nineteen had joined Jack on a concert tour of Iceland and mainland Europe, was dedicated to a life in the arts, and this didn't sit well with her grandfather. He had told her he hoped that she would move to Washington, D.C., and marry a diplomat, but instead Carol went to New York, where she studied acting at the Neighborhood Playhouse, and dance with Martha Graham, whom she came to regard as her mentor. At twenty-one she then moved to Vermont, where she later married a potter. Harry lent her the money to buy her Vermont house, and even came to visit — and eventually, among other generous acts, forgave her the debt in his will — but her talents and interests made her more a Langstaff than a Guggenheim.

In 1970 Carol was in easy reach for collaboration with her father; she had a small apartment in the South End of Boston as well as a house in Vermont. He urged her to work with him to create a new, stronger stage Revels. "He talked me into it," she says. She had already directed a Cambridge production of *Noye's Fludde* in which Jack had appeared, and he knew that her enthusiasm for ritual celebration was at least as strong as his own. He took her to Harvard University's wonderful Victorian edifice Memorial Hall and pointed out that it was the perfect place to do a Revels, and that it was empty at Christmastime.

Memorial Hall, then as now, had high stained-glass windows and a pair of great heavy doors at either end of a cavernous central marble-floored lobby, its paneled walls lined with twenty-eight tablets commemorating Harvard graduates killed in the Union army during the Civil War. On one side of the lobby was Sanders Theatre, a marvelous lecture hall with stage and curved tiers of 1,166 seats, all of it inspired by Christopher Wren's Sheldonian Theatre at the University of Oxford. On the other side was an enormous space known then as Alumni Hall, with stained-glass windows and a great vaulted roof. Today, after major renovations, it's a dining hall renamed Annenberg Hall, but in 1971 Harvard used it for everything from dances to examinations — and it would, Jack and Carol thought, make a perfect communal dressing room and backstage area.

Jack decided to make a telephone call to a friend at Harvard, Archie Epps, who was dean of students and a great music lover. Before long, Memorial Hall was available to him for two days in December — at a benevolently low rent, which rapidly grew, later, but was hugely valuable at the time. And he and Carol dived into shaping and casting the first Christmas Revels in Cambridge.

Jack told the *Orff Echo,* later:

When I first began, the idea was to start with things I had always been interested in as a layman, as a hobby: folk dancing, sword and Morris dancing, country dancing, Mummers' Plays. I thought it might be very valid to put them up on a stage or to incorporate them into a little dramatic festival. So first I imagined a theater work. But as I got more deeply into it, I recalled those days in my parents' house, and the fun of that big carol party at Christmastime. I guess I was looking for something that would touch the audience in the same way, and those participating even more. That kind of celebrating seldom happens in the formal theater.

And, of course, he wanted to satisfy the hunger for ritual that he could sense ever more clearly in the secular society around him — and in his own psyche too. As a choirboy he had felt buoyed up by the power of the church rituals in which he was taking part — but he wasn't a choirboy now. He said in another interview, with Maryn McKenna of *Boston* magazine:

> One of the only rituals we have in our country that isn't church based is that incredibly poor piece of music "Happy Birthday." Think about it. You go into a crowded restaurant and hear that tune and everyone will know what is happening — someone is celebrating an important passage in their life. That's a very powerful thing.

Now, working and planning with Carol, he began to think much more coherently about the kind of experience he wanted to create. This should be a ritual celebration of the winter solstice, a Christmas festival that — in spite of the name — was not specifically Christian or even religious. Belief should be irrelevant; if one member of a Revels audience felt she was celebrating the birth of Christ, her neighbor should be equally able to feel that he was celebrating the rebirth of the year. It should use the emotional forces of music, of dance, of words. It should be a celebration that would belong to its community, yet reach for artistic excellence. Perhaps he was reaching for a new kind of Mass, dedicated not to a specific God but to a celebration of the amazing mystery of life.

He and Carol agreed that they should use some basic material from the New York program: the Abbots Bromley Horn Dance, "The Cherry Tree Carol," Morris dances, the Mummers' Play. Jack, who had for so many years broken the rules of recital singing by talking to his audience about what they were going to hear, also wanted to abolish the fourth wall of the stage. As at the New York Masque, his Revels audience would not simply be passive, watching; they would sing. Certain carols would be part of the show; their words would be printed in the program, and at the beginning, before the house lights went down, he would come out onstage, tell the audience what they were to do, and rehearse them. He would even teach them to sing a round. In Latin. *Dona nobis pacem.* . . . In every Revels program he devised in the years ahead, "Rounds for Peace" were somewhere on the program.

He wanted children in the program, of course — and now that he had been teaching at Shady Hill for four years, he knew where to find them. The school community could also be counted on as a base for the audience, since they had all embraced him with the same devotion as the students and parents at Potomac.

And at the center of this Revels, and of every Revels thereafter, would be something that hadn't been there in the early New York or Washington productions, or on television: a large chorus, drawn from the local community. The chorus was key to Jack's whole vision of this celebration of the solstice; it was the link between performers and audience. He wanted amateurs, local amateurs, because he felt that audiences were more easily persuaded to sing if they could see a group of people just like themselves up there singing with them. But because he was also professional to the core, he wanted amateurs of professional standard. This wasn't going to be a village pageant; he wanted no allowances made.

And none were. There were — and still are — so many talented, trained, volunteer singers available in the Boston area, from the Bach Choir all the way through the alphabet to Youth pro Musica, that even the earliest Revels choruses in the 1970s sounded far better than anybody expected.

112

Jack said that Carol had ideas that would never have occurred to him.

> She's very good at opening things out, making country dancing alive, turning it into theater. Like taking the Abbots Bromley slower than they actually do in the village it comes from. In the "Apple Tree Wassail," she wanted to get apples and take them out into the audience. And she felt you should get different ages of people in, older as well as young.

So they kept this in mind when putting together their chorus, enlisting singers of all shapes and sizes, and with gray or white hair, as well as black, brown, or blond. And when Carol, as director, began blocking their onstage movements at rehearsal, she gave them an instruction that has held ever since: they should divide themselves into families. Each family held a husband, a wife, a child or children, perhaps a grandparent or two; these units would not move around the stage in self-conscious lumps, but just the awareness of the fictional relationships was enormously helpful to amateur singers who had never been taught how to behave "naturally" on a stage. Backstage, during the early Revels years, when the Memorial Hall was a single vast dressing room for the entire cast, you could see the members of each family hanging out together comfortably even when they weren't performing.

Almost everyone involved in that first 1971 Christmas Revels, except the leading musicians, was an amateur — performing, in the true meaning of the word, for love of the enterprise. Even the stage set was the work of volunteers. It was in fact not a set at all, but a vast array of small pine trees. "They brought them down from Vermont, loads of them," Jack said. "We had pine trees everywhere, all over the stage, out in the lobby, up and down Mem Hall. It was wonderful. It *smelled* like Christmas."

A high point of the program was something that was to become the fulcrum of every Revels thereafter. It was based on the Shaker song "Simple Gifts," written by a Shaker elder named Joseph Brackett in Maine, in 1848.

> 'Tis the gift to be simple, 'tis the gift to be free,
> 'Tis the gift to come down where you ought to be,
> And when we find ourselves in the place just right,
> 'Twill be in the valley of love and delight.
> When true simplicity is gain'd,
> To bow and to bend we shan't be asham'd,
> To turn, turn will be our delight,
> Till by turning, turning we come round right.

An English Quaker poet named Sydney Carter had put new words to Elder Brackett's "Simple Gifts," changing it to "The Lord of the Dance," and he recorded it in 1966, in Britain. Oddly for a Quaker, he turned the gentle statement of Shaker ideals into a beautiful metaphor that was also an overt narrative of the last days of Christ.

> I danced in the morning when the world was begun,
> And I danced in the moon and the stars and the sun,
> I came down from heaven and I danced on the earth,
> At Bethlehem I had my birth.
>
> Refrain:
> Dance, then, wherever you may be;
> I am the Lord of the Dance, said he.

And I'll lead you all wherever you may be,
And I'll lead you all in the dance, said he.

I danced for the scribe and the Pharisee,
But they would not dance and they wouldn't follow me;
I danced for the fishermen, for James and John;
They came with me and the dance went on.

I danced on the sabbath and I cured the lame,
The holy people said it was a shame;
They whipped and they stripped and they hung me high;
And they left me there on a cross to die.

I danced on a Friday when the sky turned black;
It's hard to dance with the devil on your back;
They buried my body and they thought I'd gone,
But I am the dance and I still go on.

They cut me down and I leapt up high,
I am the life that'll never, never die;
I'll live in you if you'll live in me;
I am the Lord of the Dance, said he.

From the moment Carter recorded "The Lord of the Dance," everyone tended to behave as though his words were just as much in the public domain as those of the original "Simple Gifts." Perhaps this is the crowning compliment for a writer. Jack made only a few tiny alterations when he first sang it, in the version above, but years later, cautious of offending any Jewish members of Revels audiences, he asked Carter if he might also change "on the sabbath" to "for the people" and "the holy people" to "the high and mighty." Carter, who once wrote that he believed in "nothing fixed or final," amiably told him to go ahead. Jack had known the original Shaker song all his life:

I'd done "Simple Gifts" often in concerts — and Aaron Copland put his version of it into Appalachian Spring. "The Lord of the Dance" I brought back from England, where Sydney Carter did it. I gave it to the Morris men in New York to do at a winter festival there, but it was Carol's idea to turn it into a dance combining the singer and certain figures from the Morris. So she and Shag Graetz and Jonathan Morse worked out the choreography.

"Shag" was J. Martin Graetz; he and Jonathan Morse were mainstays of the Pinewoods Morris team. So at the end of the first act of the Revels, in a quick segue, onto the stage ran four figures in Morris whites: a musician, the two dancers, and Jack, and his voice rang out as the dancers strode and leapt. It was and is a masterly piece of choreography, the movements echoing the words of the song, and the steps timed so that the Morris bells on the dancers' legs punctuate both music and meaning. For the refrain, Jack danced with the two Morris men, and the audience sang. He had duly taught them all what to do at the beginning of the show, when rehearsing them in the carols they would sing in unison at various points in the Revels. In Sanders Theatre the rafters rang.

Dance, then, wherever you may be;
I am the Lord of the Dance, said he.
And I'll lead you all wherever you may be,
And I'll lead you all in the dance, said he.

And so he did, since the lobby into which Sanders Theatre opens, now known as the Memorial Transept, is so enormous that he and Carol had decided to dance the audience into it. On the last line of the last refrain everyone onstage joined hands and Jack led them down through the house and out into this great vaulted space, collecting audience members on the way. With the brass quintet picking up the tune in a balcony, the audience found themselves singing, dancing, snaking in ever-diminishing circles until the last repeat of the refrain ended in a great communal shout. They loved it. They've loved it ever since.

Chapter Ten

"Totally in his element"

So the curtain had finally gone up on the reinvention of ritual celebration toward which Jack's life and talents had been propelling him. December 1971 was the real start of his achievement as one of the Makers. There were two performances, matinee and evening, of that first Christmas Revels; Sanders Theatre was perhaps three-quarters filled, and a cast of sixty played to a total of 1,400 people. Carol directed; Jack rehearsed all the singing. Onstage, he was the heart of the show, as a charismatic presence and a soaring voice, and it was his passionate enthusiasm for this celebration of the solstice that fired the instant devotion of performers and audiences alike.

The people who attended those two performances found a whole new kind of delight infusing their Christmas feelings, as if wine had suddenly become champagne, and they went home and told all their friends. Word spread through the Cambridge/Boston grapevine, and by the second year of the Christmas Revels, although there were still only two performances, on a single day, there were no empty seats in Sanders Theatre.

Behind the scenes, to make the first Revels actually happen, Jack and Carol enlisted a wonderfully helpful range of friends. There was Fenton Hollander, an architect with entrepreneurial instincts who later founded Water Music, to present chamber music and jazz on cruises in Boston Harbor. There was Raine Miller, then a teacher at Shady Hill, a gifted artist who began as costume designer and soon evolved into one of the major pillars of the Revels. There was, before long, an impressive array of major figures in the local arts scene offering help, advice, and/or money: Terrence Tobias, Sheppard Ferguson, Sinclair Hitchings, and many others.

"For the first Christmas Revels, David Rockefeller lent Carol five hundred dollars — so did John Lewis," Jack said. "And she managed to pay them back afterward. Graham Gund said to Raine, 'If you have any loss, I'll back it.' People were amazing, in all kinds of ways."

These were the people who made the Revels a reality, turning it from the personal vision of a single passionate artist into a powerful community institution. They wrote letters, made phone calls, drafted contracts, wrote checks; they advised and organized and schlepped. They were — and are — typical of the unsung heroes of all the artistic institutions created by the Makers. Drawn by the candle flame, these dedicated, accomplished folk devote themselves to keeping it alight. With an assortment of benevolent motives, they raise the money, they sit on the Boards, they make things happen. People rarely write books about them, but without them, books like this one could never be written, because there would be no story to tell.

Jack was the same polymath he had been before, teaching at Shady Hill, performing, working on picture books based on folk songs, speaking at educational conferences on the place of live music in a school curriculum. Now he had to incorporate a lot more into this complex pattern: all the letters and meetings and phone calls that would help raise the money and enlist the performers and production staff for the next Christmas Revels, and the next. Fund-raising was never his favorite occupation: Carol remembers a meeting with a wealthy couple at which, in spite of their constant inquiries about how they could help, Jack could never bring himself to stop describing his ideas for Revels and actually ask for money. On occasion he also had to force himself to listen to cautionary or even negative advice from the more experienced of his volunteer advisers, which was a little like trying to mute the sparkling of a very lively firework.

In 1973, with Nancy thriving as a teacher at the Cambridge Friends School, he gave up his post as music director at Shady Hill, causing almost as much mourning among students and parents as he had at Potomac. Instead he went to a little office on Joy Street, on Boston's Beacon Hill, to become the New England director of Young Audiences, a job that would prove to make a useful contribution of its own to the development of the Revels. He enjoyed it enormously, he reported.

Young Audiences is a national nonprofit organization for bringing the performing arts into schools. I work with terrific young musicians, actors, and dancers on special programs for this, and I help them to develop ways to relate their presentation to kids, and actually involve the students in their music, et cetera.

Young Audiences Arts for Learning, as it's now known, was founded in 1952, and reaches seven million schoolchildren a year through affiliates in more than thirty cities. In the arts-deprived schools of today's economy it's probably even more valuable than it was then. Performances and workshops bring live drama, painting, music, and verse to kids with starved imaginations fed only by images on screens. Jack loved his new job; his missionary zeal blossomed on Joy Street just as it always had in classrooms. And as a nonprofit, Young Audiences taught him about the difficulties of raising money for the arts, particularly from foundations and government agencies. Above all it gave him the chance to hunt out, hear, and see even more of the talented performers working in New England than he knew already. Over the years, the best of them would turn up not just in schools lucky enough to be served by Young Audiences, but on the Sanders Theatre stage at a Revels.

Carol was his collaborator in these early Christmas Revels, but she was also Mrs. Peter Duveneck, raising small children on a farm in South Strafford, Vermont, four hours' drive from Lexington or Cambridge. Part of her artistic ethos was and is a very strong sense of "earth and community," and it was beginning to tug her imagination to Vermont rather than Sanders Theatre. She and Jack still worked closely together, however, and they collaborated on a book for Doubleday, a collection of street games and rhymes called *Shimmy Shimmy Coke-Ca-Pop!* ("Bring a yo-yo, a bouncing ball, your hula hoop, and your skip rope," ran their instructions to children attending an outdoor celebration based on the book, at the Newton Free Library, near Boston.) And their shared sense of ritual led them, after the success of the first two Christmas Revels, to add another Revels celebrating the spring.

Christmas and Easter, the two great festivals of the Christian calendar, had been the peaks of the singing year for Jack as a choir-boy. His Christmas Revels employed not only the name but much of the music of the Christian festival, even though he always took care to stress that it was rooted in the far-older celebration of the winter solstice, the shortest day of the year, when sunlight begins at last to take back the hours muffled by the winter dark. But his Spring Revels had very little connection with the Christian Easter; it was a joyous celebration of the new life of all green things and all creatures, and it was held in May, the time of the spring fire festival of the Celts, called Beltane.

Sanders Theatre being otherwise occupied in May of 1974, the first Spring Revels was held at Kresge, the big auditorium of the Massachusetts Institute of Technology. It was filled with music and dance for the greening of the year, and Carol had chorus members running into the audience to hand out daffodils. Like every Christmas Revels, it had a focal point at the end of the first act, drawing the members of the audience to their feet to dance and sing. At Christmas this magic was worked by *The Lord of the Dance,* in spring by the ritual of the Padstow Hobby Horse, otherwise known as the Obby Oss. Led by Jack, the Morris men, and the masked figure of the Oss, out came the audience into the green field surrounding Kresge, jigging and singing in delight.

> *Unite and unite, now let us unite,*
> *For summer is a-come in today,*
> *And whither we are going, we all will unite,*
> *In the merry morning of May. . . .*

This was the kind of thing Jack always loved: a theatrical simplification of a cheery ritual that has been taking over the town of Padstow, in North Cornwall, every May for as long as anyone can

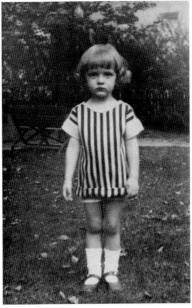

*John Meredith Langstaff, in Brooklyn
Heights, New York, circa 1923*

Jack with his brothers, Ken and David, on Christmas Eve, 1927

Above: Jack, Ken, their sister, Esther ("Terry"), and David

Left: Meredith and Esther Langstaff with the three boys

Dr. Walter Russell Bowie, rector of Grace Episcopal Church, New York

The choirboy: Jack (front right, with Ken) lived at Grace Church Choir School for five years, starting at age seven.

From left: Ken, an unidentified friend, and Jack at the camp in Bretton Woods, New Hampshire, where they sang every summer

"He made a lasting impression on me." Jack with his folk dance mentor Douglas Kennedy

Jack and Diane Guggenheim Langstaff, 1943

"It is not often that one encounters a young singer with such a natural gift for music,"
said the New York Times.

Right: Teaching folk song to members of the Country Dance Society at Pinewoods Camp, Plymouth, Massachusetts

Below: Conducting British school-children for the BBC television series Making Music

Jack with his daughter Deborah

The Potomac School, McLean, Virginia, where Jack taught for twelve years. "The whole school turns itself to music" wrote a student.

Young Carol Langstaff, with dulcimer

Jack as Noye in the first U.S. production of Britten's Noye's Fludde, *at the Potomac School*

Gary, Deborah, John, Nancy, and Jack

Sibling reunion: Jack, Terry, David, and Ken Langstaff

At one of the first Revels in Cambridge, Massachusetts

Jack and the Revels cast head offstage to collect the audience for The Lord of the Dance

The peak of a Christmas Revels: conducting chorus and audience in The Sussex Mummers' Carol

Cracking up the cast of a Washington Revels at dress rehearsal

Nancy

Jack

Jack with Dmitri Pokrovsky (center) and Patrick Swanson, 1990

Rehearsing a Cambridge Revels, with David Coffin (center right) and chorus

With friends at the celebration of Revels' 25th anniversary in 1995: Jack, Gayle Rich, and George Emlen

Left to right: Jerome Epstein, Kate Grant, Susan Cooper, Jack, Jean Ritchie, and Ifeanyi Menkiti

Carol and Jack revisiting Sanders Theatre

Jack and Sir George Martin revisiting the studio where Martin first recorded Jack — and thirteen years later, the Beatles

"Sing — *sing!*"

remember. (There's another one in South Cornwall, the Helston Furry Dance, but with a Mummers Play called *Hal-An-Tow* instead of the Oss.) The roots of the Padstow Maying go down into the mythic soil shared by those of the Green Man, of all May Day ceremonies, and all the variants of spring sacrifice listed in James Frazer's *The Golden Bough*. Today it's performed for fun, but as Jack instinctively knew, the subconscious compulsion that keeps it going is still the ritual celebration of death and rebirth.

The Oss looks rather like a circular black tent, with a man's masked head emerging from its flat top, and his dancing feet visible underneath; a "Teaser" dances with and around it. At the end of each verse of the "Maying Song" it droops down and "dies," to be revived again as the chorus roars into the refrain, *Unite and unite.* . . . In Padstow itself there are in fact two Osses, dancing their way through the streets in separate processions; the whole village is decked with flowers and flags and everyone wears white, so that the whole place seems to be filled with Morris men.

Jack didn't go quite this far, but he kept the bouncing musical accompaniment of accordion, drum, and sometimes brass — and also the Oss's trick of making an unexpected tilting rush to trap the nearest pretty girl under its black tentlike robe. In Padstow, tradition has it that any girl caught even for a moment by the Oss will be married or pregnant before the year is out, but this didn't appear in the Revels' program notes.

The Spring Revels had immediate and joyful audiences among all the weary New Englanders who had survived their six months of winter. It was clear to everyone concerned with the show, from Jack and Carol on down, that they would have to do it again the next year. So now there were two complicated new theatrical institutions to be kept going. Soon there would in fact be three, since Carol's belief in the power of community was driving her to establish the first of many offshoots: Revels North, in Hanover, New Hampshire, presenting a parallel Christmas Revels at the Hopkins Center on the Dartmouth campus.

The Christmas Revels was a regular event at Sanders Theatre now, each year brilliant but brief: the 1974 Revels consisted of three performances crowded into one day. Production costs inevitably rose as the shows multiplied, but Jack was firmly opposed to raising ticket prices, which in those distant days were $3 for an adult and $1.50 for a child. There was no commercial motive behind this enterprise; he would have made Revels performances free if he could. Reality caught up with him, however, through the forceful reasoning of his collaborators; if he wanted a nonprofit enterprise, they pointed out, Revels would have to be legally registered as such.

Carol says, "We really had to talk Dad into incorporating — it was hard for him to swallow. He didn't want a board; he wanted to keep it a Mom-and-Pop thing. But Fenton and I had been running Revels through my checkbook, and that couldn't go on."

So Jack's brainchild was incorporated under the laws of the Commonwealth of Massachusetts as Revels, Inc., "a nonprofit tax-exempt educational organization to further the production of The Christmas Revels and The Spring Revels and related projects."

This was a key time for Revels. If it had been based on a warm, fuzzy idea in the head of a dilettante, it would have had a small local success among aficionados and then faded away. But the immediate audience response proved that it did indeed fulfill what Jack had described as "this need — the lack of opportunity in people's lives to have any communal celebration." And because he was at heart a professional, with determinedly high standards, in his several separate worlds he inspired not just admiration but respect. Soon there was a growing list of benevolent Friends of Revels, who

124

made their annual tax-deductible donations and had their names gratefully listed in the program in return. And before long, the first grant came from the National Endowment for the Arts, describing Revels as "a new and different form of musical theater."

Ironically, for an institution based primarily on goodwill but almost belligerently non-Christian, the first foothold of Revels was in a church (and is again today, when the thriving hub of Revels, Inc., occupies a floor of offices owned by St. John's Church in Watertown, a mile or two up the road from Cambridge). After an initial year or two of what Jack described as "tickets all over the bed," Revels set up a tiny office in the basement of the First Congregational Church in Cambridge — which also contained a large meeting room in which the early Revels choruses rehearsed. Known as "First Church," this handsome brick church with a rooster on its tower is actually Victorian, but in 1633, looking rather different, it really was the first church in Cambridge.

This was the home of Revels' mostly voluntary staff for years, though the rehearsals soon migrated to the hall of a public elementary school, the Peabody School, half a mile away. Jack wore a little track between the First Church, his Young Audiences office in Boston, and the Lexington house where he still lived — with Nancy, her piano and her harpsichord, his sprawling collection of books and music, his beehives and his grapes, and sometimes the now college-age children. At the end of each Revels season, after the months of preparation and rehearsal and the brief exuberant day or two crammed with performances, the Lexington house was the scene of a joyous party for cast and crew. Chorus members and volunteers ate, drank, sang, and danced their way through the small low-ceilinged rooms of the eighteenth-century house until their energy ran out. It was like an enormous family party.

Nancy stood in a doorway watching them all, at one of these

parties in the 1970s. It was very late, and she probably had to teach the next day. Jack was in the midst of the crowd, his arms raised to conduct the music as he laughed and sang, and she looked at him with a smile that was enormously affectionate and perhaps a little rueful.

"There's Jack, *totally* in his element," she said.

CHAPTER ELEVEN

THE RECRUITING SERGEANT

s Maker of the Revels, Jack Langstaff had to deal with more complicated situations than he did as singer or teacher. Revels itself was complicated, being nonprofit and incorporating a great many amateurs. He had to maintain its identity as an essentially communal celebration but at the same time reassure his professional principals that they were taking part in an enterprise with seriously high standards. He also had to woo them with a serious fee, particularly if they belonged to one of the musicians' unions. For a man who hated making direct requests, all this took persuasiveness, charm, and his own particular brand of apologetic diplomacy.

Wooing musicians took the least effort; most of them were already his friends. For his soloists, in the beginning he needed early musicians, since the first few Revels were set in a more or less medieval England, with the robes of the chorus giving rich color to the wooden paneling of Sanders Theatre's stage. Luckily Boston was then on its way to becoming the early music capital of the world; its celebrated Early Music Festival wasn't founded until 1980, but the talented musicians were gathering. Most of them had their beginnings in the Quadrivium, an extraordinary combination of voices and early instruments created by Marleen Montgomery, and Jack knew them all. So it was Marleen's group and its offshoots that brought the eerie purity of early music to a lot of Revels audience members who had never even heard of a shawm or a krummhorn or a sackbut.

The offshoots founded by members of Quadrivium included legendary groups like Alexander's Feast, Libana, and Voice of the Turtle, and all of them became beloved staples of Revels for the next three decades. Carol Langstaff says that it was Jack who put together the musicians who made up Alexander's Feast, using them initially for the schools served by Young Audiences and later for Revels. Tolerant and devoted, all these early musicians sang, played, and did almost anything Jack asked — even, in the case of the tenor John Fleagle, to the point of undergoing stark terror.

John had one of the most beautiful tenor voices I have ever heard, with the same unearthly quality as the English singer Peter Pears; he also had wavy golden-brown hair and looked like a Florentine angel. At Christmas 1987, Jack indeed requested him to become an angel: to sing, *a cappella,* the fourteenth-century carol "Angelus ad Virginem" from the top balcony of the stage as part of an experimental Revels that became known as The Light and the Dark.

"The theater will be dark," Jack said to him eagerly, describing his vision, "and then we hear conch shells blowing, and the sounds of the wind, and the sea — and poetry ending 'And all about the courtly stable / Bright-harnessed Angels stand in order serviceable' — and then suddenly we see you up there, spotlit, singing! It'll be great!"

128

John didn't show quite the same enthusiasm for this prospect, but he was a trouper, and he loved Jack. He nodded.

What Jack hadn't yet mentioned was that John wouldn't simply be singing from the stage balcony; he'd be hanging from it.

And there John was, when the time came and his lovely voice pealed through the theater: a gleaming winged angel, shrouded in mist, suspended in the air above the dark stage. Part of the magic was of course due to the stage crew who operated the great helium-filled wings, the dry ice producing the mist, and the harness that kept the angel from crashing to the hard stage floor fifteen feet below. But mostly it belonged to John, and his devotion to his artistic director. What *he* hadn't mentioned to Jack was that he was absolutely terrified of heights.

One of the most versatile of the early musicians didn't need to be recruited; he volunteered. David Coffin wrote to Jack from New York asking if he could be in a Revels because he longed to play the tune for the Abbots Bromley Horn Dance, and he couldn't think of anywhere else to play it. Jack put him in touch with Carol, and the next year David duly performed in her Hanover Revels. The year after that he moved to Boston, and although he was sent a letter inviting him to be in the Cambridge Revels, he was also asked to audition.

The same thing happened the next year, and the next. I sort of resented having to audition each year, having already sung solos and played instruments, so I decided to sing the same song at each year's audition — "Four Green Fields." After four years of this Jack started singing the song with me — and I never had to audition again. . . . Onstage, Jack always seemed to be floating just a few inches off the floor. His very presence elevated him, and we all held our heads high just to see him, to sing with him. You wanted to sing with him, you couldn't help yourself.

There were plenty of people in the world of folk music and dance who wanted to join Jack too, after his decades of singing and dancing with the Country Dance and Song Society. May Gadd, grande dame of the society, had just retired after decades as its director, and Jack lured her to the fourth Cambridge Revels and listed her on the program as Traditional Dance Director and Consultant. The Pinewoods Morris Men, one of the best teams on either side of the Atlantic, had been a basic part of Revels ever since their members Shag Graetz and Jonathan Morse had joined Carol in devising the choreography for "The Lord of the Dance," and they came back almost every year. Among the dozens of cast members in the vast dressing room of Memorial Hall, they tended to keep to themselves, and were deeply respected for their capacity for beer.

Pinewoods and the CDSS also provided Jack with Jerome Epstein, who lived and worked in New York but from 1970 onward came to accompany him whenever and wherever he gave a folk-song concert. One of Jack's most devoted friends, Jerry became a familiar presence on Revels stages with his concertina or accordion, and he rapidly grew accustomed to regular phone calls from Jack requesting a new arrangement of a song or carol. (Another Revels arranger was an even older friend, Nancy's sister, Marshall, by now known as Marshall Barron.) Jerry helped bring the Revels to New York in 1979, and was its music director there for fifteen years.

Nearly everybody found Jack's enthusiasm irresistible; he launched into relationships as eagerly as he sang a new song. Another musician who found himself answering requests for arrangements was the horn player/composer/physicist Brian Holmes, who was part of the excellent Cambridge Symphonic Brass quintet hired for every Revels from 1974 onward. Jack loved to use the brass for a rousing overture, which Brian generally wrote, and for its power in the dramatic build of a carol sung with the audience. Brian remembers his enthusiasm as having the intensity of a teenager.

His voice is a permanent feature of my mental landscape, that sweet baritone—and his way of offering positive feedback on everything. And that enthusiasm . . . sometimes it went beyond what was practical. I remember standing with him and the producer on the stage of Sanders a week before a Revels was to open, and Jack announcing that he wanted me to write a descant trumpet part to be played from the balcony. The producer cringed, since this would have increased the cost of the brass by about twenty percent.

Though Brian eventually moved away from Cambridge, he went on writing for Jack—and playing his horn in Revels, which by then had spread to both his subsequent homes, New York and California. Today, as a composer, he finds that a third of all the music he has written is connected with Christmas. "In some ways Jack has been like a father to me," he says.

He didn't specifically interact with me as a composer—I think that because his image of Revels came from his experience with folk song, he wanted his material to be authentic. I remember he told me several times not to put major seventh chords into the arrangements—that wouldn't have been authentic, I guess. But I would put them in anyway and he always praised the arrangements, so maybe he didn't mind. Or maybe he didn't notice. . . .

Brian Holmes thinks back to standing onstage at Revels intermissions and "playing my horn to help the audience along" while Jack taught them to sing the "Sussex Mummers' Carol." He thinks back to visiting Jack the summer before he died, and finding him working hard to finish the Revels book of sea chanteys. He says, remembering, "It was like warming my hands in front of a fire to see him again."

One of the first nonmusicians Jack recruited was Robert J. Lurtsema, known to listeners of Boston's WGBH-FM and other public radio stations as Robert J. He was a local celebrity. Quirky and self-confident, Lurtsema was a classical disc jockey who since 1971 had run a program called *Morning Pro Musica* for five hours every morning, seven days a week. He had a voice like dark chocolate and was known for beginning his program with several minutes of unannounced birdsong, indulging in long pregnant pauses, reading his own news bulletins, and expanding the program to include live studio performances and interviews. Carol had met Lurtsema through the folk scene of the sixties, when she was singing at Club 47 and he was running a radio folk show. So she called him, and he interviewed her and Jack on WGBH. Jack admired Lurtsema's speaking voice and knowledge of music and guessed, rightly, that he had an itch to perform.

So he said, "Bob, I wonder if . . ."

Before long Robert J. was a regular part of the Christmas Revels, declaiming the only two pieces of prose or verse Jack had ever included: a few lines from *Hamlet,* and a truncated quotation from the sixteenth-century priest-architect Fra Giovanni Giocondo:

I salute you! There is nothing I can give you which you have not; but there is much that, while I cannot give, you can take.

132

No heaven can come to us unless our hearts find rest in it today. Take Heaven.

No peace lies in the future which is not hidden in this present instant. Take Peace.

The gloom of the world is but a shadow; behind it, yet within our reach, is joy. Take Joy.

And so, at this Christmastime, I greet you, with the prayer that for you, now and forever, the day breaks and the shadows flee away.

Lurtsema also played Father Christmas in the Mummers' Play, whose cast was truly community-based and included a wild variety of talents from the chorus. Being short, balding, and rotund, with a fringe of gray beard, he made a highly suitable Father Christmas — and took pride in earning a round of startled applause at each performance by turning a cartwheel across the stage. At the first rehearsal, this surprised even Jack; he hadn't known that in Robert J.'s versatile youth, before he settled down and became a magisterial radio voice, he had briefly been a trapeze artist in a circus.

Jack's recruiting instinct never slept; he was always ready to reach out to someone who might be useful to Revels. At which point, this narrative has to switch into the first person, since my own recruitment was a classic example of the Langstaff technique.

I first set eyes on Jack Langstaff in 1974, eleven years after I married an American and moved from London to the United States. Chronically homesick for Britain and its layered past, I had just finished writing the fourth in a sequence of five myth-haunted fantasies called *The Dark Is Rising;* they dealt with the powers of the Light and the Dark, though set in the real world. One book was shaped by the winter solstice and the twelve days of Christmas; another included a spring carnival based on the Padstow May Day celebrations. I'd never heard of Jack or his Revels.

One day in December my New York editor, Margaret K. McElderry, came to stay, and we went to the Christmas Revels at Sanders Theatre. We were all entranced, especially my children, Jon and Kate, aged seven and five. Since Margaret was also Jack's editor, she insisted on taking us backstage to meet him.

"But I've read your books!" cried Jack, shaking my hand. "You should be writing for the Revels!"

"I'd love to," I said, still on a Christmas Revels high.

He looked at me more closely. "Really?"

"Really. But what could I write?"

"I'll be in touch," he said.

About six weeks later, sometime in February 1975, he came to call on me, bringing Raine Miller with him. The Revels budget then was still tiny, and a large part of it went to the rental of the theater; sets were still minimal, and Raine had become legendary for the glowing medieval costumes that she contrived out of next to nothing. She looked a little like someone from a medieval painting herself, with flowing brocade garments and long straight hair. It soon became apparent that she was the more practical member of this team, acting as a kind of sea anchor to Jack's flights of imagination.

Jack said to me, "Do you know *Sir Gawain and the Green Knight?*"

"Well, as it happens —" I went to the bookshelves and produced the Tolkien & Gordon edition of the original Middle English text, heavily annotated in my nineteen-year-old hand. After battling with compulsory Anglo-Saxon at university, it had been almost a treat to learn Middle English.

"I thought it might be fun to have a dramatized version in the next Christmas Revels," he said.

"Great," I said. "Would you like me to try?"

"Do you really think you could find the time? It's a lot to ask, I know how busy you are — I wouldn't want to overload you —"

He went on like this for several minutes, intent and concerned. It was his modus operandi, though I hadn't learned that yet: instinctively he made requests with such self-deprecating reluctance that it would have seemed deeply churlish to deny him what he needed.

Raine said to me, "We have a terribly small budget."

"Oh, well now," said Jack, embarrassed. "I'm sure we . . . I know you must . . . We can come to some . . ."

"That's all right," I said cheerfully. "You can't afford me. Let's not bother about money."

"Oh, my," said Jack. "Oh, come now — we can't possibly —"

Raine grinned. "OK," she said. "Thanks."

"The *Gawain*'s rather long, of course," Jack said, suddenly down-to-earth again. "Maybe just do the first half. Then if they like it, we could do the second half next year."

So I became a Revels person. That's how people were said to become part of the Revels in those early days, and no doubt still are; it's a matter of personal chemistry, a subjective judgment. Someone could be a talented singer, a natural performer, a skilled manager, but in the end there was always the same question: "Is he — or she — a Revels person?" The only time I can recall the answer seeming perhaps to be no was in the case of a researcher who became one of our producers, whose manner was so diffident and academic that it took her years to stop addressing Jack as "Mr. Langstaff "— and she turned out to be so good at everything that she was clearly a Revels person *inside*.

135

Jack recruited people who shared his own attitudes. A "Revels person" had to have enthusiasm, dedication, an instinctive emotional response to traditional material — but above all a respect for it. People who liked simply to dress up in tights or robes for a Renaissance Fayre and play at being Elizabethan did not qualify for a place in a Revels cast, though he was perfectly happy to have them in the audience. A Revels was fun, but at its heart was something deeply serious. Like all ritual, it was not to be treated lightly.

I duly turned the first half of *Sir Gawain* into a kind of play-poem, and it was staged within the 1975 Christmas Revels by Esquire Jauchem and his Boston Repertory Theatre, whom Jack had already recruited while wearing his Young Audiences hat. The following year, we did the second half. And somehow, in the course of that twelve months, I became Jack's tame writer for the next twenty years.

Perhaps he needed one more collaborator. He still relied on Carol to devise each show with him, but she was also busy in Vermont with a Revels of her own. (In 1976 there were four performances of the Christmas Revels in Cambridge and two in Hanover.) Up to this point, he had never even had a script for any Revels: just a running order, with a collection of photocopied pieces of music for the chorus. Wherever he went, he was carrying a battered briefcase with paper spilling out of it. His car was full of paper; I sometimes felt his car was his real office. He made barely legible notes on envelopes, on the backs of letters, on cocktail napkins, and was always hunting for them.

Nancy tried to help keep his life in order, but her own was increasingly busy. Raine Miller tried too; by now she had left Shady Hill School to run a small preschool in her Cambridge house, and her spare time overflowed with work for Revels. Besides designing and making costumes, she kept track of all of Jack's Revels ideas and commitments and was his highly competent liaison with practically everybody.

That left the planning of the material. Jack came calling again.

"Susan — about spring. Do you know Howard Pyle?"

"American illustrator, yes? Children's books?"

"Robin Hood!" said Jack, with a nostalgic gleam in his eye. "He did a wonderful Robin Hood, I used to love it. You know all those stories, of course you know all those stories. I'll bring you my copy."

"Little John . . . Friar Tuck . . . Allan a Dale . . . D'you want me to turn one of them into a play?"

"Well, if you have . . . I know how busy you are . . . If you really think you . . ."

We decided on a short play about Robin Hood and Little John, and he began listing the things he wanted to fit into the next Spring Revels. He was like a Roman candle, fizzing with ideas.

"A Scots pipe band, wouldn't that be wonderful? And Scottish dancing, there's this amazing group . . . and a great Indian sitar player called Peter Row, and some wonderful dancers . . . and Tony Barrand and John Roberts and their lovely pub songs . . . and that great gospel hymn 'Shall We Gather at the River?' — and Purcell's 'Bartholomew Fair' — and do you know 'Nottamun Town'? . . ."

He half sang a couple of lines of it, in that breathy sketch sound that real singers use in order to spare the Voice. It was a haunting tune and I'd never heard it before. Jack had been singing it for decades; he'd recorded it in London when I was still in high school.

He said, "But I'm having trouble with the shape. . . . I wonder if you . . ."

So we began a sort of talking tennis game that evolved into a narrative form for the next spring show. So far, each Revels had been a collection of rather disparate musical elements, but Jack's theatrical instinct made him want to give them a shape. In his usual indirect manner, he asked for some verse passages to frame the songs and dances he wanted to use, and there were other casual requests along the way.

"'The Lyke Wake Dirge' — it's very long and it's all in old Scots — could you simplify it?"

"Sure."

"And the Feast can do 'Miri It Is.' You might need to write some new words. . . ."

This tennis game went on at intervals until Jack — simultaneously discussing everything with Carol — was happy with the form of his Revels, and on my little Olivetti portable typewriter I tapped out not just the things I'd written but, for the heck of it, the text of the entire show. Nobody had ever had time to do this before, and the stage management team were delighted to have a real script that they could annotate with lighting, moves, entrances, and so on. We didn't have many copies in 1977, however, because Revels couldn't afford the photocopying bill.

In my files, the typefaces of the Revels scripts change, year by year, from typewriter to word processor to computer, because I went on doing all this — joining the planning debates, typing the script, writing lyrics, plays, and the program notes, for Christmas and Spring Revels — until around 1995. Like all Jack's enormous professional family, I'd been recruited. I was a Revels person, for life.

For that Spring Revels with the Robin Hood play, he changed someone else's life as well. Patrick Swanson, known as Paddy, was an accomplished young English actor-director who had recently come to the U.S. with his girlfriend, Danielle. "In the spirit of adventure" they had answered an ad in the *Boston Globe* for a couple to run an organic farm owned by a doctor.

One evening when Paddy came in from his chores, the doctor, Josephine, told him that her clinic had been visited by a group of singers sent by Young Audiences to sing music from *The Magic Flute* to the patients. She had been chatting to a very nice man who was looking for a Robin Hood, she said, and she had told him that she had one at her farm. The next morning, Paddy found himself at the local school, where the same group was to perform.

And Jack Langstaff intercepted me as I came into the room. "Hallo," he said. "Here's a place, sit down here and listen to this. Children like Papageno. Look at them! Josie has told me all about you. You don't mind if we sit here, do you?" We sat on the floor surrounded by ten-year-olds, and as a Magic Flute *aria filled the room the conversation went on in an urgent whisper. "Of course you probably won't be able to do this, I know you have the cows to milk — how did you learn to do that? — Josie told me, but we have this play about Robin Hood and Little John and I have a good actor who could do Little John and it would be wonderful to have an English Robin. . . . Oh, by the way, there's a Morris team who could do the Padstow May ceremony — do you know about that? — and outside the theater there's a grassy area and I thought someday we might do a sheepshearing. You don't know where we might find a sheepshearer, do you? . . ."*

So there was Paddy, a few months later, onstage at Sanders Theatre playing Robin Hood:

— and singing, among other things, a mysterious ballad called "Nottamun Town." I shared the stage with a chorus of volunteer singers, a gaggle of children, two English balladeers, a group of Indian musicians, a Morris dancing side, a Spanish dance company, three ewes, and a lamb. I had come

under the influence of Jack Langstaff and the spirit of his creation — the Revels.

And he stayed there, first as actor and then, increasingly, as a director, and when Jack retired as Artistic Director in 1995, Paddy Swanson took his place.

Jack's memory was a lucky bag of talented performers. For certain kinds of British folk song he would bring in Robin Howard, the actress-singer with whom he had toured in *Voyages* during the 1960s; she had a strong, beautiful, faintly Irish voice. For pub songs or sea chanteys he enlisted Tony Barrand and John Roberts, whom he knew from Pinewoods: two transplanted English singer-dancer-teachers who had linked up at Cornell, and whose wonderful repertoire of folk song, from classic to bawdy, masked a couple of doctorates in psychology. And a plan to do a Revels based on Victorian and Edwardian material produced an instant string of names:

Ron Smedley, that's who we need. Ron Smedley, countryman of yours. And David Jones, you must know David. And that marvelous Irishwoman in New Bedford, Maggi Peirce — you've heard Maggi —

He always expected the members of his many small worlds to know the members of all the rest. Within each of those worlds — lieder, choral music, folk song, music teaching, children's books, Revels — everyone did indeed know everyone else, but Jack was the only one who crossed all the boundaries. He had heard Maggi Peirce sing at her coffeehouse in New Bedford, Massachusetts. She came from Belfast, had an all-embracing motherly smile, called us all darlin', and looked like the personification of British music hall.

David Jones was from Jack's folk-song world, another great performer of traditional British songs and chanteys; he came from London and sounded just like my dad.

As for Ron Smedley, he still lived in London; Jack had met him in the 1960s while working on his BBC TV series *Making Music.* Television administration was Ron's day job. His true love was dance, in all its forms, and he taught at the Royal Ballet School and directed the enormous festivals that the English Folk Dance Society held each year at the Royal Albert Hall. When he eventually turned up in Cambridge, Massachusetts, for rehearsals, he began teaching selected members of the chorus the hilarious "animal dances" from ragtime America — the Bunny Hug, the Turkey Trot — which had outraged conservative English Edwardians around 1910, and the delight of his dancers was wonderful to see. They couldn't stop smiling when they made their way home from rehearsals. Nor could we; nor, in due course, could the audiences. The sight of dignified, beautifully gowned and tailored ladies and gentlemen suddenly kicking up their heels to a jingly string band was a high point of the seventh Christmas Revels.

One by one, with each Revels that went by, the team of Revels people grew. Those of us working backstage became a permanent family, with Jack as the paternal connection: so did some of the individual performers and groups, and a talented central core of the chorus. And everything began to grow. Jack increased the number of performances to five, and reluctantly raised the ticket prices to $2 for children and $4 for adults. The demand for tickets was huge; in 1977 all five performances sold out, and four thousand ticket orders had to be returned unfulfilled.

Since very few of those orders were for a single ticket, and since Sanders Theatre holds more than a thousand, that meant that we could probably have sold out at least six more performances. But we couldn't afford it; we were still a shoestring operation. Even for a gorgeously costumed production, Raine's costume budget was $850 — about $7 per costume. I still can't imagine how she did it.

As the Cambridge Revels grew, Carol's Revels North was thriving. While still contributing hugely to the content and nature of the Cambridge shows, she was directing not only the Christmas Revels in Hanover but a summer Country Revels in Strafford, Vermont, and taking a small performing company to summer farmers' markets. Revels North gave three or four Christmas performances, in those days often using the same script as Cambridge and some of the same artists, particularly Jack and Alexander's Feast. There was a great deal of traffic between the northern and southern Revels, sometimes in terrible weather. Gayle Rich was once summoned in an emergency to drive a carload of fake snow to the Hanover production — and ran into a blinding snowstorm on the way.

Jack's trips were often eventful as well, since his mind was always in so many places at once that his driving became legendary. I had a phone call from him one winter at some wholly unexpected time of day, and I asked where he was.

"Well," said Jack reluctantly. "Well . . . there's nothing wrong, but I'm in this hospital. . . . There was just this little incident with the car. . . ."

He had hit a deer, driving back from Hanover, and the car was a total loss. Deer are of course a familiar hazard of winter driving in New England, so it wasn't his fault. Perhaps it was never his fault. I do remember, though, the expression on my small son Jon's face one day after Jack had given him a ride home from school. "Mummy," he said in wonder, "when Mr. Langstaff is talking, sometimes he goes very fast and sometimes he goes very slow, and *sometimes he takes both hands off the wheel!*"

Jack's approach to professional matters was also idiosyncratic, though less perilous. He was a delight to work with, but he was not easy, or direct. In his own quiet way he was profoundly obstinate, but he hated confrontation. It was a virtue and a vice. Though he would occasionally admit to being angry—"I am very provoked!" he would say—he would wriggle like a worm in sunlight to avoid a fight.

He even had a problem uttering any negative criticism. I learned over the years that I could gauge his true opinion of something I'd written only by listening to the *degree* of his enthusiasm. A direct negative statement wouldn't do, for Jack—which could lead to misunderstandings. Gayle Rich, who became the Executive Director of Revels, and who is a wise woman, once said, "Right from the beginning I have always seen myself as Jack's translator."

But when there was something he wanted, it was very hard to stop him.

One day, before rehearsals began for a Spring Revels, Jack said to me, "I'm going to use your English words for 'L'Homme Armé,' they *fit* so well."

Since he was so often indirect, this sounded a little like an introduction.

"Ah," I said carefully, waiting to see what might be coming next.

"And I want to end with that wonderful Mennonite hymn, you know—'We Are Going Down the Valley.'"

"Great."

"I just wondered if you could rewrite the words."

"*What?*"

"Well, it's such a downer. I mean, listen:

We are going down the valley one by one,
With our faces tow'rd the setting of the sun;

143

Down the valley where the mournful cypress grows,
Where the stream of death in silence onward flows."

He was right, it certainly wasn't cheerful.

He said, "Couldn't you make it the *rising* of the sun?"

"But, Jack, it's a classic. People would freak. It's like asking me to rewrite 'God Save the Queen.'"

Jack grinned. "We've already done that over here," he said. "It's called 'My Country, 'Tis of Thee.'"

So of course I did what he wanted. We all did, always, in the end.

We are going down the valley one by one,
Dawn is breaking and the day has just begun;
We are free of all the terrors of the night
And ahead of us the eastern sky is bright:
We are going down the valley, going down the valley,
Going toward the rising of the sun.

Carol's Hanover stage manager, a true Revels person, was so dedicated to theater that he persuaded Jack to let him come and help stage-manage at Sanders; he was an enchanting young man named Winthrop Bean, known as Winkie, who made friends wherever he went. Winkie was cheerful, talented, highly intelligent, and quietly iconoclastic; at his high-school graduation he secretly gave each member of his class a glass marble, which they were instructed to transfer to the palm of the headmaster as they crossed the stage and shook his hand. We never found out how the poor headmaster coped with all the marbles.

When working with Jack, Winkie kept his imaginative powers focused on the stage; he was particularly creative when making props, and was clearly headed for a lively career in stage design. By

1979 he was the Revels stage manager not only in Cambridge but in New York. Almost twenty years after Jack's first New York Revels at Town Hall, a dedicated group led by Jack's brother Ken and Jerry Epstein had brought it back to the city again—this time to the Upper West Side, for three days at St. Paul's Chapel at Columbia University. Early in the proceedings Jack managed to put his foot through the boards of the special stage being erected in the chapel and sprained his ankle, but this didn't stop him from giving three performances—and four days later, seven more in Cambridge.

Winkie Bean moved to New York, like so many young theater hopefuls. But both Revels and the stage lost him, because one night in 1983 he was brutally murdered on a New York street. The show that Christmas in Cambridge was a Slavic Revels directed by Carol, as lively as Winkie himself had always been. Jack wrote a muted dedication paragraph for the program:

> We dedicate this Revels to our young friend Winthrop Bean, who, with us, envisioned this special production. He was killed this year before he could help us mount this show, but many of the imaginative props he created for Revels are on stage.

"It's not enough," he said, looking at what he'd written. "But what could anyone possibly say that would be enough?"

CHAPTER TWELVE

FIFTY IDEAS BEFORE BREAKFAST

*J*ack had been busy before, but now he was a man in perpetual motion; he always had so many plans and ideas bouncing around his head that no day ever seemed quite long enough. (Nancy Langstaff once observed that she dreaded his reading the daily newspaper, because it would produce fifty new ideas before breakfast.) Certainly no day was quite like the last or the next, and if he wasn't occupied with work for Young Audiences or Revels, his flow of energy swiftly curved around to a new book, or an Orff-based way of teaching children music, or plans to visit a labyrinth in an obscure part of Belgium.

The projects were never predictable; nor was the range of the people in his life. Finding once that we had a few unoccupied hours at a literary conference in Oxford, he whisked me off to have tea at Christ Church College with a religious friend who was about to retreat from the world into an enclosed Carthusian order in France.

She was a genial lady who had just come back from six months' solitude in Alaska. I never did discover where or how they had met.

The senior Langstaff siblings were still close, Jack and Ken in particular, and there was a growing generation of younger Langstaffs; inevitably all of them were musical, though not always by occupation. After two decades of international business experience, Ken had settled down with a firm of extremely high-level headhunters, and was living in Stamford, Connecticut. His eldest son, David, was at Harvard and already singing in the Cambridge Revels; before long he was one of its producers too, and he has played an important background — and sometimes onstage — role in Revels ever since.

Jack's own immediate family was as important a part of his life as it had ever been, though they could probably only be sure of his continuous presence and attention if they were all in some remote, peaceful family retreat. At first this was "the island," which meant Pomquet Island, off the coast of Nova Scotia, a tiny islet that Jack had bought one day on impulse, sight unseen, after learning that the Crown Commissioners were calling for sealed bids to sell off former lighthouse islands. It was, says Deborah, one of his totally crazy ideas that turned out to be a wonderful thing.

> *My mother had a fit, since it was more than twenty-four hours from home, uninhabited, and cost something like twelve hundred dollars, which was a lot to spend on a lark! But we all loved it, and we'd go tenting there for weeks at a time, swimming off the rocks, cooking over fires, sharing the woods with the great blue heron colony.*

Before ten years were out, there was another crazy-wonderful idea, though this time it was a family enterprise, and lasted far longer;

they all built a cabin on a hillside in Vermont. It was a very Langstaff idea: the communal creation of something that would become the home of a summer family gathering—a kind of ritual. Off they all went from Lexington to Vermont with their tents and tools, one summer in the late 1970s: Jack, Nancy, John, Gary, Deborah, the boys' girlfriends, and a permutation of friends who would stay for a few days to help. Deborah was about twenty-three; she had worked for a year as a carpenter, so she oversaw the construction—with, she says, a lot of help from her brothers.

There was lots of communal head-scratching and figuring things out when we got to challenging junctures. Local carpenters came to inspect us, nodding in amazed approval. John did the plumbing. We all did everything: measuring, sawing, hammering, getting up on the roof, making rustic furniture . . . It rained a lot that summer, and we were there for a month. It was a beautiful time together, working, talking, laughing, having meals, falling into bed at the end of the day. And a summer week or two there became our family gathering time and place—not Thanksgiving or Christmas, as with so many other families. It was wonderful.

Jack, the performer, the endlessly active Maker, loved to escape into the tranquillity and simplicity of both places. The Vermont cabin and the island overlapped for a few years, and I have a letter he wrote to me from Pomquet Island in the summer of 1979:

We are at the mercy of the elements and primitive living— boiling our drinking water, firewood from the woods, mussels from the shoals, sunlight only source for reading by, no contact with the mainland for food or post unless the ocean is

calm enough to row. But we are surrounded with beauty and
wonderful life — the enormous expanse of sea, changes in sky,
ocean, and winds, as well as the gorgeous seabirds that live
here with us.

Then at once there follow two pages of detailed suggestions of songs and dances that he felt we should consider for the following winter's Christmas Revels. To mail this letter, he had rowed to the mainland and back in a very small dinghy. Even in his remote, peaceful wilderness the ebullience of his creative imagination wouldn't let him rest.

To feed that imagination, Jack had a phenomenal memory for songs and sources, and his research was indefatigable. All year long, he would burrow into obscure books from assorted libraries, make copies of every reference he could find, and send me batches of them annotated in his unmistakable handwriting, which always looked as if a very busy insect had been leaping inky-footed about the page. Sometimes he forgot to take the books back, and uncomplainingly paid amazingly large library fines. (His only similar expenditure was on parking tickets.) The list of the songs and dances he wanted to include in each show was always two or three times longer than we had time for; never, ever, was there a shortage of material.

Revels was the primary object of this constant flow of ideas; along with his deep respect for all things traditional, Jack had an aversion to boring repetition. His audience's comfortable acceptance of the Christmas Revels as a sequence of medieval words, song, and dance was, for him, the signal that it was time to do something different. This had been the major impulse behind the Victorian Revels for which he imported Ron Smedley and which was as much fun as any Revels before or since. Perhaps it was the nearest he ever came to reproducing his delight in the Langstaff family carol parties —

which had their roots in the same period, since both his parents had been born in the reign of Queen Victoria.

He made that Revels a kind of magical distillation of the nineteenth-century Christmas, a rival for any of those endless dramatizations of Dickens's *A Christmas Carol* that pop up annually all over the United States. Indeed the magic embraced each audience before they even reached the theater. Jack managed to enlist the Cambridge Salvation Army band for the show, and Raine Miller found somewhere in storage — to the amazement of the band — a set of the original Army uniforms from the turn of the century. So as the audiences arrived at Sanders Theatre, there in the snow stood a nineteenth-century Sally Army playing carols to greet them, taking them back in time before they'd even entered the theater's very Victorian doors.

Using the real band was a classic example of Jack's principle of community celebration, and the musicians themselves had a great time. They manfully turned up for four of the year's five performances, and at the Saturday matinee, which they couldn't manage, Brian Holmes led a substitute group of professional musicians whom Jack happily labeled in the program the Bram Stoker Ad Hoc Brass Sextet. Devising imaginative names for performing groups within each Revels was one of his trademarks, and he came up with some gleeful London names that year: the Tottenham Criers, the Pudding Lane Waits, the Strand Singers, the Pickwick Mummers, the Dingley Dell Dancers, and Fezziwig's Parlour Players.

He began this Revels with the closest thing to a stage set that his designers could manage on the cramped Sanders Theatre stage: it became a London street, with glowing shop fronts (painted by Raine Miller's mother, also an artist), simulated gas lamps, and a pub sign. When he had finished his usual preshow ritual of teaching the audience the carols they would eventually sing, he brought down the houselights and turned the stage to dusk, and out of the wings, silently, came the lamplighter with his long pole, to light the "gas lamps." Members of the chorus began drifting onstage, and down the aisles in all parts of the audience, street criers came wandering, a succession of plaintive or robust voices hawking their wares. *Chairs to mend, old chairs to mend. . . .* There was no shortage of street cries; Jack had already published a whole book of them. Then suddenly with a great cheerful blast of sound, the Salvation Army band came marching down the center aisle playing "Hark! The Herald Angels Sing," and the audience was singing too and the Revels had begun.

There were music hall songs in the lively, Cockney first act, rocking the audience with a variety of nineteenth-century pop music that most of them had never heard before. And when the Lord of Misrule was dragged from the audience, he was enrobed not as a medieval lord but as a Cockney Pearly King — thanks to a saintly volunteer named Susan Yates, who sewed thousands of little pearl buttons onto a jacket in the tradition of East London's Pearly King and Queen. But it was the second act that became the echo of Jack's childhood, though set back some twenty years: it was a Christmas carol party complete with host.

This time the host wasn't Meredith Langstaff but his son, in white tie and tails, and there were a thousand guests out there in the Sanders Theatre audience. Revels' stage crew had an unusually busy intermission, and the street scene became a Christmas drawing room with children decorating a tree. It was an upscale party; a small orchestra was playing onstage while the arriving chorus-member guests were greeted not only by their host but by a butler. But then, the audiences and choruses of Revels tended to be fairly well up the scale in terms of income and education too. Jack did what he could to broaden their range, and brought in city schoolchildren free to watch the dress rehearsals, but his theater was after all part of an

Ivy League university, in the most prosperous part of Cambridge, Massachusetts. Even the onstage butler was played by Charles "Chuck" Hammond, the curator of Gore Place, one of the Boston area's stately homes.

And there's my favorite Revels story, concerning the performance of this Victorian Revels before which the tailcoat of one of the tallest chorus members went missing. Raine Miller, on impulse, went running out into the streets around Sanders Theatre and started banging on front doors.

"Please," she cried when the first one opened, "can you lend Revels a tailcoat?"

The man who opened the door smiled at her. He was not only a world-famous economist, he was six feet-eight inches tall. "Certainly," said John Kenneth Galbraith.

After the carols and dances of the onstage party, and a send-up of Dickens called *The Sorry Tale of Jacob Marley* ("Can you do a piece of drama?" Jack had said hopefully), the jewel of this second act came from another one of the more unexpected Langstaff recruits. Somehow, Jack had found and enlisted a wonderful paper-sculptor named Jim Bottomley to make props representing every single object mentioned in the carol "The Twelve Days of Christmas." Jim designed them, and for three months a team of volunteers had helped him to make them, every single one, from the partridge in the pear tree to the twelve drummers drumming. They were large and lifelike and all the same color: silver.

The audience sang the carol in a state of mounting amazement, as magnificent gleaming props were danced in with every verse, and a great silver mound grew in the center of the stage. It glittered there magically through the climactic "Sussex Mummers Carol," and through the cheers for the cast's curtain call, and since Sanders Theatre has neither proscenium nor curtain, there it stayed until the last member of the audience had left. As they all pulled on their coats and shepherded their children out of the theater, you could see their heads turn back toward the stage for one last look, before they went out into the snow.

And the Salvation Army band serenaded them on their way home.

The mail from devoted audience members that year, Jack reported, was almost equally divided between those who called the Victorian Revels the best ever, and those who mourned their peaceful Renaissance program. "That's a healthy mix," he said with satisfaction, and proceeded to design a Revels for the following spring that would be even further from the Renaissance, focused on ships and the sea. Against all advice, he insisted on having a great forty-foot mast raised onstage during the singing of sea chanteys; the local fire department was very nervous, and the audience was delighted.

Before you could say knife, he was bubbling with ideas for a Revels that would be predominantly French. He wrote in a letter:

Not to distract you, but I've written to Claude Roche-Fogarty (Black Wheat Theatre) in France; and I'm looking about for something that could be used at Christmas from the conte-fable *of the Middle Ages. Heard about a book by an Englishman, Russell Hope Robbins, a translation of the Old French* Les Cent Nouvelles Nouvelles, *which I must look up. The Arthurian Sir Gawain has French roots too, doesn't it? . . .*

He added that he had some wonderful French music for the Quadrivium and the Voice of the Turtle, that he would like the Mummers' Play put into Franglais, a Chartres Cathedral stained-glass window projected onto a scrim, French tapestries hung onstage, and the windows of Sanders Theatre lit from outside by the fire department. And, he said, it would be great to have John Fleagle sing the thirteenth-century *Orientis Partibus,* a mock celebration of the Flight from Egypt, known as "the song of the ass," with a real donkey onstage.

Remembering the backstage habits of the live ewes he and Carol had put onstage in one Spring Revels, I wrote back:

Oh, Jack. Dear heart. Real sheep we managed, a real mast we managed — but this year you'll be singing in Hanover AND New York AND Cambridge AND you want a real donkey?

He did indeed sing in three different cities in succession that year, but for the French Revels in Cambridge we managed to dissuade him from including the donkey — he made do with a couple of hawks, borrowed from the Boston Children's Museum. One of his other ideas, however, was to end the show with a sixteenth-century French carol called "Sing We Noel," which he had never used before.

The tune was beautiful, and he wanted an English lyric for it. I began it *Over the snowy hill the travelers go.* . . . and wrote three verses; words and music were printed in the program, as are all Revels songs intended to be sung *tutti,* and the audience was rehearsed by Jack at the top of the act. It's a heady experience to hear a thousand people singing words you have written, and I would stand at the back of the theater for the show's climax, feeling an extra Christmas glow as the last verse rang out. But Revels was an institution by now, and its audiences were accustomed to the climax of their Christmas ritual being the "Sussex Mummers Carol." They felt deprived. One night, having finished "Sing We Noel," they went right on and sang the "Sussex Mummers" anyway.

The ideas went bubbling on. He came up with a lively Afro-

154

Anglo-American Revels one spring, enlisting a talented Boston company called the Art of Black Dance and the brilliant jazz saxophonist Stan Strickland, who has been a mainstay of Revels programs ever since. The following year he added the singer Bessie Jones and some of her Georgia Sea Island Singers, first recorded by Alan Lomax, for an even livelier show. There were several Sea Revels, a Celtic Revels, and an Appalachian Revels that he built around the memories and voice of the folksinger Jean Ritchie. And once he came up with a Christmas Revels that was a startling breakaway from the others, the result of an idea taken to an extreme.

A remarkable number of the children to whom Jack had taught music at the Potomac School grew up to be very interesting people, and one of them was Christopher Janney. He studied architecture and music and then did a master's degree in environmental art at MIT; his thesis project became a wonderful installation at the Boston Museum of Science called *Soundstair*, in which light and sound are triggered by — and as a result, affect — your movements as you walk up or down a flight of stairs. Since then he has created all manner of marvels, mostly in public spaces like airports — though one of the most celebrated was his 1998 *Heartbeat*, in which Mikhail Baryshnikov danced to the varying beat of his own heart. In 1987 Jack conceived the notion of getting together with Chris, me, and the avant-garde composer David Moss to create a Christmas Revels that would combine sound, music, and words on the theme of the Light and the Dark. The result was controversial, but managed to express two of Jack's lifelong passions: the Everyman quality of his favorite figure in all myth and folklore, the Fool; and the deep conviction that whatever conflict and destruction mankind may bring upon itself and the planet, somehow, in the end, all will be well.

This was the Revels that included John Fleagle's perilous and beautiful moment as a flying angel. Jack also broke with tradition by

155

giving it a Mummers' Play performed in silence, by mimes. Above all, though, it was a reiteration of the Quaker-like pattern he loved to use in Revels, of spreading peace over man-made chaos. Its climax involved not only the entire cast but more technology than any Revels before or since:

Ghostly in half-dark, with the chorus lost in shadow at the back of the stage, the Morris men and the mimes have moved through the Abbots Bromley Horn Dance, and as they disappear, just one of them, David Zucker as the Fool, is left onstage. And things change.

Alone onstage in the dim light, the Fool has a little pair of cymbals in his hand; he strikes it, once. Listens to it. In the air, there's a child's voice, over a background of playground noises, children laughing, it says:

I wish I wish this wish for you
I wish I wish your dream come true;
I wish I wish this wish beside —
You may not see the nightmare ride. . . .

And in a red light we see children playing, laughing, batting a balloon to and fro. The Fool strikes his cymbals again for them, more flamboyantly, and as if in response, light onstage begins to grow, and with it a sound of voices saying hundreds of words that we can't yet quite hear, layers of words. (They are on tape, but the live chorus is echoing them.)

Behold, I show you a mystery. . . .
They shall have stars at elbow and foot. . . .
What wondrous life is this I lead? . . .
This is the key of the Kingdom.
Of the Kingdom this is the key. . . .

156

And on and on, line after line, including a number from T. S. Eliot's *Four Quartets.* The voices fill the air, continuous, overlapping.

The Fool strikes his cymbals again, again, pleased and proud, and we see that the growing light comes from a great sun starting to glow behind him. The children are gone but he doesn't notice. He finds that the high sweep of his arm makes the voices louder; pleased, he does it again, reaching up, and they respond.

The sun grows brighter, brighter, and proudly the Fool brings it on, striking his cymbals, reaching to make the voices louder — to a point where the whole theater is bright with the blaze of this blinding, round sun. Then the sound of the Fool's cymbals is picked up on tape, deeper, louder — and suddenly drowned, in the deafening boom of a great bell.

The sound is overwhelming, and a black edge of shadow begins to creep over the sun's giant disk. The Fool panics, cowering, clutching his cymbals to silence them, but he can't stop the sound. It grows and grows, the layered taped words — different, darker words now — running faster, deeper, denser, with a drone from the chorus beneath, and the light fades as the eclipse swallows the sun.

The Fool spins around, arms wide, in an appeal for help, but he finds a chaos of small bright points of light around him (the chorus, whirling about with a light in each hand) in the growing dark — and then the eclipse is total. A red ring surrounds the black sun, the whirling lights engulf the Fool, and the chaos of noise is like a great terrible apocalypse.

Then gradually the whirling lights onstage grow still,

moving into three clusters, and through the appalling noise the audience begins to hear music, the sound of voices singing "Dona Nobis Pacem."

There are chorus members out in the house as well as on stage, singing their hearts out, and the audience picks up the timing from them and begins to sing too, in the three divisions that Jack gave them at intermission. And gradually, gradually, the music quells the chaos that the Fool's hubris has produced. As they all sing, the noise begins to die and the light begins to return; the black disc and the red ring fade away and all you can hear is the whole house singing, and every light in the place is up full, flooding the house and the stage.

Jack is at center stage now, conducting, and he brings the voices down, softer, softer, *pianissimo,* until the song is no more than a whisper. The children run across the stage, playing, unaware, as they had at the beginning, and over the last of the song comes the clear childish voice we heard before:

I wish I wish this wish for you

I wish I wish your dream come true . . .

And suddenly the air is filled with dancing golden points of light, so that you can hear the people in the audience catch their breath as they look up. It is one more touch from Chris Janney: the release of tiny pieces of gold Mylar from the top balconies of Sanders Theatre.

Then — to return to reality and the past tense — a trumpet sounded, and they all launched into "Sing We Noel." And the audience wasn't deprived of their "Sussex Mummers' Carol" because Jack and the cast led them out into the cavernous lobby and everyone sang it there — discovering that Chris had planted the whole lobby with reminders of magic, his effect called *Reach,* so that if they were in the right place they could reach up an arm, like the Fool, and trigger a chord of music out of the air.

When they first heard about the shower of gold, the more practical Revels people had protested. Sanders Theatre would have to be laboriously swept free of little gold Mylar flakes, they pointed out, after every performance.

"No, it won't," Jack said. "You wait. Chris says the audience will take them home."

And he was right: they did.

One other moment from that show was pure Jack, even though he wasn't there to witness it. Before and after each performance, bells tolled out from the tower of Sanders Theatre — not real bells, but a tape Chris Janney had made of the bells of Lincoln Cathedral, in England. Access to the tower had been limited since it was badly damaged in a fire in 1956, but one night after the show Chris took me up to the point where he had installed his speakers.

"Look," he said. "Just look!"

So we looked down from the tower, as the bells pealed out into the cold air. Snow had been falling, and all the roofs and streets of Cambridge were white. Way below us, writing their footsteps on the snow, people were streaming out of the theater in couples and groups, muffled and booted, going home to glowing Christmas trees and expectant stockings. There were no cars to be seen; you wouldn't have been surprised if a Dickensian horse and carriage had come jingling into view. It was a wonderful picture of Christmas, classic, timeless, impossible to forget. It was . . . well, it was the Christmas Revels.

CHAPTER THIRTEEN

MASTER OF THE REVELS

*J*ack was still a good fit as director of the New England branch of Young Audiences; he had all the right talents, not just to discover bright young artists, but to help them devise ways of grabbing the imaginations of audiences in schools. He enjoyed working with them, and he certainly enjoyed finding them. But by 1981, he was so deeply occupied with Revels, and was brimming with so many plans for its future, that the Revels Board managed enough creative fund-raising to offer him the paid post of Artistic Director. Though the salary was only $20,000, it was enough to allow him to give up his day job.

He wrote a letter to the Board of Young Audiences:

Dear Members of the Board,
      It is not without difficulty that I have decided to terminate my work with Young Audiences. As you know, the other

half of my professional work has been in graduate teaching, my own concert work, and direction of the Revels, which has grown incredibly since I first produced it. Revels, Inc., is at a crucial point now where the Board has asked me to take on a full-time job as it expands its outreach, publications, recordings, education, and research. If I don't go into this fully, the new directions can't be realized. It is a tremendous challenge. . . .

The concept of Young Audiences is one I will always believe in, and my admiration for what you are doing to make it work is steadfast. It has been a pleasure working not only for you, but with you.

He remained something of a nomad; this was still the period when one felt his real desk was the paper-littered backseat of his car. The official home of Revels, Inc., was still the little space in the basement of the First Church, near Harvard Square, but now it had a paid staff of three: Jack as Artistic Director, Raine as Artistic Coordinator, Beth Wilbur as Business Manager. The Board of Directors, on which Jack and Carol both sat, met regularly to guide the future. They argued a lot, often about Jack's artistic decisions, but it was probably the work of those solidly practical early people that turned Revels into a viable organization.

But the Cambridge shows were multiplying, and now Revels was making records too; for the first of them, Jack had taken a hand-picked chorus into Sanders Theatre and invited an audience as well, so that the recording would sound like a live Revels performance. After that he used Harvard's Paine Hall, which is smaller. The recordings too began to multiply; now there was another company, Revels Records, and the conducting was shared by Jack, George Emlen, and Jerry Epstein.

George Emlen, musician and choral conductor, who is now as essential to the music of Revels as Jack once was, is a Revels person whom Jack first recruited without even knowing it. George was teaching in Maine when he and his wife first heard about the Revels in the mid-1970s.

We didn't know Sanders Theatre, and we asked for seats in the front row. So our first experience of Jack, as for so many, was having this joyous presence burst onstage, thrust out his hands to us, and cry, "Sing! Sing!" We were bowled over. We went backstage and met him. . . . and from then on became die-hard Revels fans. I staged a Revels-like event at the College of the Atlantic, where I was teaching, and I think the thing that most impressed Jack was the fact that we'd done it for two hundred dollars.

Over the years, George visited Jack at the Young Audiences office, and in 1980, a year after getting a graduate degree in choral conducting from the New England Conservatory of Music, he went to a "How to Revel" workshop given by Jack, Carol, and Raine at Andover. By that time he scarcely needed the workshop. Jack's recruiting instinct was already at work.

He loved the fact that as well as sharing his classical background, I'd played accordion in a contra dance band, and called the dances. And in 1984, when I came down to sign a contract to teach at Noble and Greenough School, I stopped in at a rehearsal of the Sea Revels in the Old South Church. I told Jack that I was going to be in Boston, and he said, "Good! Now you can direct the chorus!" So I've been doing it ever since.

Since Jack had neither the time nor the energy to come up with a totally new concept for each year's Revels, there was now a certain amount of duplication; Cambridge scripts were used in other cities (with emissaries sent to report on them, since Jack was much concerned with quality control as the Revels name spread), and the Cambridge company itself performed revised versions of the Victorian, Anglo-French, and Appalachian Revels. But the audiences enjoyed the repetition, and the shows still sold out — and one repeat of a Spring Revels was illuminated by two stories from New England's master storyteller Jay O'Callahan.

Jack recognized a kindred spirit right away; he invited Jay back to Revels several times after that, and the two of them made a CD together called *Stories and Sea Songs*. They were both at the National Storytelling Festival at Washington College in rural Tennessee in 1985, and Jay remembers seeing Jack faced with a challenging roomful of seasoned storytellers, magicians all in their own way. What did he do? "He gathered everyone in a circle, turned the lights off, and sang 'Wild Mountain Thyme,'" Jay said. "Storytellers all over the country still remember it. No one remembers what we talked about that week. They call it the 'Wild Mountain Thyme' conference."

He also remembers the archetypal Langstaff reaction when he showed Jack the room where he was to stay for the conference. "Washington College was on lean times. I showed Jack his room. His window was broken, his cot sagged, the walls were cracked, and there was nowhere to hang his clothes. Jack looked out the window. 'Cows!' he said. 'Great! And right by my window. Great!'"

By 1986 there were four other Revels companies, in Hanover, New York, Washington, D.C., and California, and their dates were staggered so that Jack could perform in all of them. Inquiries about starting similar celebrations had come in from Maine, Virginia,

Washington, Ohio, Colorado, Texas, and British Columbia. The year-round pressures of Revels and all the rest of his singing and teaching life multiplied. Nudged by his family, his friends, and his board, he began shifting responsibilities, and in the course of the 1980s George Emlen became Music Director, Paddy Swanson became Associate Artistic Director, and Gayle Rich became General Manager. Revels acquired a proper set of offices overlooking a loading dock at 1 Kendall Square, Cambridge, near MIT, and a permanent staff of five. Over the next seven years, it gradually became clear that Jack was aiming the organization toward a point where he could leave and devote himself to all his other projects.

But not just yet. He hadn't finished. For one thing, there was an unfulfilled idea for a Christmas Revels that he had been talking about for years. Each time there had been the same conversation.

"Children's books. Come on, Susan. A Storybook Revels. Something to do with children's literature."

"You've always had children in the show — the games, all those songs —"

"Yes, yes, but *children's books* . . . There just has be a way to do it."

"I don't know how."

"Neither do I. It's very provoking."

But there came a point when he was so determined to make this happen that we did find a way; it was the only time a Revels took on the shape of a play. The script was full of characters from classic children's books, starting with a magician and his boy helper who perform the puppet play of *St. George and the Dragon* at a party in Edwardian London (another echo of those Langstaff carol parties). Visually, the puppet theater would be a copy of a Pollock's Toy Theatre, idiosyncratic Victorian paper cutouts that Jack used to love buying on visits to London.

At a crucial point in the performance, the Boy finds he has lost the St. George puppet, and the Magician, furious, banishes him on a quest to find St. George. There's a blackout, with lightning and thunder, and suddenly we are inside the puppet theater. The Sanders stage has become a Pollock's proscenium, and within it the Boy finds himself with the puppet characters from the play, now life-size — including the magnificent Dragon.

The Dragon roars off in pursuit of all the other characters — except the Fool. He is a mime (Jack had used a wonderful mime, Trent Arterberry, in several previous Revels, and this show was written for Trent to double the parts of the Fool and the Magician). With him, and of course with the audience, the Boy sets off through the Land of Storybook, to find St. George, and the Revels becomes his quest.

Once Jack had approved the script, the real work began. Many people exerted much time and effort to raise money: this was a high-budget show, like the Light and the Dark Revels the previous year. The designers began work on costumes, masks, props — even the prop list for this Revels was two pages long, single-spaced. And Jack managed to persuade Trina Schart Hyman to design the proscenium for the Pollock's Theatre, which was no mean feat; Trina was not only a Caldecott Medal winner but one of the best and busiest artists in the world of children's books, and an outspoken lady with firm opinions.

Jack, the set designer Eric Levenson, and I drove up to see her in New Hampshire, we all talked a great deal, and eventually Trina sent Jack a beautifully detailed design for a proscenium arch, all twining trees and vines. He brought it to Eric, Raine Miller, and me and we all studied it. It was perfect — almost.

"There's just one thing," Jack said. "Look at those rabbits."

At the foot of each pillar of the arch were some adorable little bunny rabbits. They looked so real you wanted to stroke their velvety ears.

"Cute," said Eric drily.

"Eeuuw," said Raine. "They've got to go."

Jack said carefully, "I'm afraid they're not exactly . . . I hope Trina won't be offended, but . . . Susan, maybe you could write to her."

"Me?" I said in horror.

"Well, you know her . . . you're both authors . . . you'd know *just* what to say."

So with enormous reluctance I composed a letter to Trina, all about the exigencies of theatrical collaboration and the myth-based nature of Revels and please would she mind getting rid of the bunnies. It took a long time.

On August 31 Trina wrote back. Her letters were always elegant and unmistakable, written with a fine black pen in little narrow capital letters; only the "Trina" at the bottom was ever in script.

Dear Susan,

Of course I don't mind. I say "of course" although my first reaction was to be very pissed off — so I put your letter aside for a day until your sentence "I shouldn't dream of interfering if this were a book . . ." had a chance to sink in. You are quite right; in the theater things are interdependent. Besides which, this isn't really the most creative or personal project for me. (I still don't know quite why I'm doing it at all — I was, as I think I said, quite satisfied with the Christmas Revels as they were ten years ago — but I suppose time marches on, and creative innovation must have its day, and Jack is such a bulldozer personality that he carries all along in his path. I

actually have no idea why I'm doing this, and actually I <u>hate</u>
doing "vegetation," although nowhere near as much as I hate
drawing horses. Do you know what I mean? Do people ever
say to you, "Oh, do us a dark fantasy, Susan — you're so <u>good</u>
at it!"? Which is the only reason why I wanted to put some-
thing <u>else</u> in there.) So, I shall do whatever you think is best,
honestly; no problem.

But if Jack doesn't send that proscenium puppet-theater
mock-up along to me very soon, all this agonizing will be for
naught — I'm starting work on a book October 1st, and once
I've started a book, I'm <u>gone</u>. Which I'm sure you know about
too. . . .

It was good to see you, and thanks for writing that letter.
I know it wasn't easy, and you did it well.

Best, Trina

Three weeks later she sent us the finished design. It looked wonderful; the rabbits had gone and the cover letter came, as Jack said,
from a true Revels person.

Dear Eric, Jack, and Susan,

I think this is more or less what you wanted for the fan-
tasy proscenium arch. In case you hadn't noticed, the tree
branches coming together around the moon is also an echo of
the ring of swords that lop off St. George's head. (Sometimes I
can't help myself.)

Eric, I know you'll understand that you're to adapt this as
you see fit. I know that colors may have to be simplified and
shapes altered to get this thing to work at a distance. Never
having had to work for distance, as you can see, I'm bad at

it. The important effect is the intertwining branches working toward the moon. I guess. What about using silvered Mylar for the circle of the moon? Or is that too tacky? In any case, do with it what you will. If this is completely off base and stupid, just tell me what to do next.

The panels are — or will be — as you see from the sketches.

I'd love to just throw glitter over this whole thing. I should have joined the circus long ago.

Best, Trina

Eric and his crew built the set, and it looked wonderful.

The script involved a Storyteller, a disembodied voice; the actor Hume Cronyn, with whom I'd worked for years in my other, non-Revels life, agreed to play it for us. He came to Cambridge to tape the voice-over, being as fond of Jack as the rest of us were. Jack sent him a fee, and Hume sent it right back as a donation to Revels.

December came, and the first performance. After a splendid overture written for brass by George Emlen, Hume's quiet story-telling voice filled the theater to set the scene:

"Once upon a time." That's the way every good story begins. Now, the story I am going to tell you is about a boy on a midwinter's quest, and it starts — but only starts — in London, in England.

And out of the carol party, the story rolled its magical way through incident and song; past Merlyn, past the Green Knight, past the looming giant of "The False Knight in the Road," sung by Jack, past Robin Howard as the Old Woman Who Lived in a Shoe, and all her singing children, past David Coffin as the Pied Piper. Merlyn had given the Boy a riddle to follow, but it wasn't helping him much.

> *Look at him and you shall see*
> *Your ally and your enemy;*
> *His face is hard for you to find,*
> *Harder yet his secret mind,*
> *Yet when all his heart you know*
> *Safely through the world you'll go.*

In "The Lord of the Dance" Jack took the Boy's hand as he danced down to lead the audience out, making our small Everyman the link between performers and audience. And through more storybook incidents and some masterly mime devised by Trent, the Boy followed his quest until at last he found himself among a crowd watching the Mummers' Play.

The play took its traditional course, the Dragon killed the Turkish Knight — and the Boy was happy and expectant, knowing that now at last he would find St. George, because this was the moment for the hero of the play to come to the rescue.

Here's the script. Father Christmas says, as always:

> *St. George shall come and die by swords*
> *Which circle round his neck;*
> *As Winter dies, so shall he die,*
> *And then to life again like Spring!*

The Boy is peering offstage like everyone else, waiting anxiously for St. George to enter. But as he peers, every other person onstage turns his or her head deliberately to look at him. Still staring, they move a step or two away from him, isolating him. The stage lights go down, all but a spot on the Boy.

169

And the Fool comes to the Boy, carrying a sword and shield and a small white tabard with a red cross. The Boy stares at him, puzzled. The Fool puts the tabard over the Boy's head and the sword and shield into his hands. Then he kneels briefly at the Boy's feet.

And in Sanders Theatre there was a soft *Oh* sound from the audience as they realized, like the Boy, that he himself had to be St. George. Jack said it was his favorite moment in the show. It was mine too: somehow I'd always thought of my Boy as an echo of choirboy Jack.

So the Boy was St. George. There was a splendid dragon fight ("Look out, St. George!" cried a child's voice from the audience at one crucial moment); the Boy slew the Dragon, the Morris men slew the Boy; the Fool revived him with a magic sprig of mistletoe. The Boy sat up and began to sing:

Good morning, gentlemen,
A-sleeping I have been. . . .

Suddenly the Fool swung a cloak around his shoulders and was the Magician again, and he pulled off the Boy's tabard, crumpled it, and handed it back to him — and lo, it was a St. George puppet. There was a great flash of light, a crash of thunder, and stage and theater were suddenly dark for a second time as the Revels crew worked like demons to achieve their own magical change of scene. And, said the script:

From the speakers, on tape, we hear the Boy's voice softly singing the last words of his final verse as St. George.

. . . The dancers shall have a dance
And the mummers have their pay!

The stage lights go up, and we are back in the Victorian Christmas party. Beside the little stage of the puppet theater the Magician and his Boy are bowing, as the guests applaud them.

The voice comes conversationally over the speakers once more.

STORYTELLER

So our tale is done.

And who is to say whether the people on one stage are more real than the people on another? Once upon a time, a boy achieved a midwinter quest, and began the long business of growing up. Once upon a time, a family celebrated a rather unusual Christmas in Victorian London. Once upon a time, a thousand people filled a midwinter theater in Cambridge, Massachusetts, and lived, for a while, inside a story, once upon a time. . . .

Jack had announced that this Revels would be his last. It had been seamlessly directed by Melodie Arterberry, who like her mime husband, Trent, had a long-standing association with Jack and the Revels, and it was dedicated to the memory of Marleen Montgomery, who had died untimely that year. Jack wrote to the cast and crew:

Let me tell you again how much <u>this</u> Revels meant to me, because of each of you and what you did to make it all happen — my fellow singers, dancers, musicians, our production staff and team in every aspect of the show . . . It was my last in Cambridge, and I can't think of a more beautiful production in which to end my performing here. Many of

you will carry on this Cambridge tradition, and I'm sure we
will meet again in other productions at some future time.
You all made the midwinter quest — now safely through
the world you'll go. . . .
With all good wishes to each of you.
In friendship's name,
Jack

He didn't retire, of course; he just stopped performing in Cambridge — in order to perform in the other cities. He was still Artistic Director of Revels, Inc., and his Revels family was still expanding; Philadelphia, Pennsylvania, was about to become the sixth. After that, Houston, Texas, would become the seventh, thanks largely to the continued enthusiasm of Jack's nephew David, now a successful Texas-based entrepreneur.

A copy of Jack's schedule for the fall and winter of 1989 shows him zigzagging between the cities of Cambridge, New York, Philadelphia, and San Francisco. Every month he visited all four, sometimes with Paddy or George: in September for chorus auditions; in October for production meetings; in November for rehearsals; in December for performances. He devoted particular time and care to Philadelphia, this being its first Revels — and on the way from Philadelphia rehearsals to San Francisco rehearsals, he made a side trip to the opening night of the Revels in Washington, D.C. He was about to have his seventieth birthday, and from time to time there were pains in his chest, and he paid neither of these facts any attention at all.

He still had one more long-cherished idea to accomplish. He had been trying to make it happen for years; it was a Russian Revels, and he managed to bring it both to California and Cambridge in

1990 — a year after the Berlin Wall came down, and a year before the USSR broke up.

Jack had discovered Dmitri Pokrovsky when he first visited the U.S. in 1988; he was a musician, conductor, folk-song collector, the father of the seventies revival of folk song and dance in the USSR They had been planning to collaborate ever since, but the process was long and painfully slow. As the Sanders Theatre program eventually put it: "By mail and fax and recalcitrant telephone (and the occasional exchange of text hand-delivered by people like the Ensemble's American representative, Abigail Adams, or the Revels' assistant producer, Kate Grant, who spent last year living in the Soviet Union), work went on for two years to make a Russian-and-American Revels a reality here and in San Francisco."

Though Dmitri was twenty years younger than Jack, the two men were astoundingly similar: dedicated, charismatic performer-teachers who generated instant enthusiasm and affection in their choruses. They had the same ebullience, the same urge for communication, and of course the same passion for folk song. When we all first met in 1990 it was wonderful to watch them talking nonstop to each other, like two rivers tumbling into the same course.

Born in 1944, Dmitri had grown up in the bleak Communist culture personified by all those elephantine stone statues of Soviet Hero Tractor Driver. He studied music — principally balalaika and orchestral conducting — in Moscow and graduated as a classical musician. But, he said, when we were all getting to know one another:

As a balalaika player, I couldn't understand where the music was for me to play. I hated what was called "Russian folk song"; it was awful music. In the thirties, you see, the authorities had said, "We must get rid of the kulak *culture, there will be no more peasants, instead we have workers." So in music as in all the other arts, they replaced everything with this workers' culture, and the real folk song had gone.*

It hadn't really gone, though; it was still surviving underground. In the summer of 1969 Pokrovsky, by then teaching classes in conducting at the October Revolution School of Music, went off on a trip to Archangelsk, in the far north of Russia.

There was the midnight sun, you know? Kids playing football at two o'clock in the morning. And outside a house I heard this amazing sound, music like I had never heard before, and I found five old women sitting on a bench singing folk song. I can still see them, outdoors there, singing. It was the real Russian folk song, from the old days — the old people had kept it alive.

So he and his students began to collect these hidden treasures. In villages and country districts all over the huge republic of Russia, they sought out singers and musicians — some of them amazingly good — who still privately played and sang the hymns, carols, ballads, and ritual material forbidden since Stalin's time. It was a slow process, since the country people were often suspicious and nervous, and the government was hardly likely to approve; the "workers' culture" of the Soviet Union had no use for ethnomusicologists.

But Dmitri and his researchers persisted, laboriously recording endless improvisations of songs and dances never written down before; eventually they had more than two thousand, and a lot of original folk costumes and early musical instruments as well. The

Pokrovsky Ensemble became first a school of folksinging and then a performance group, touring cities all over Russia, taking Russian folk music back to the people whose hidden heritage it had always been. They had to wait for the arrival of Gorbachev and *glasnost* to be able to take it to the rest of the world.

As Dmitri and Jack talked and talked in Cambridge, it rapidly became clear that there were striking similarities not just between the two men but between the two sets of folk material they spent their lives translating into performance. Both cultures had North European roots; both were focused on the winter solstice. Nearly everything was based on the image of darkness swallowing the old year, and the need for propitiation so that light would return as the new year was born. Our Anglo-American culture had had waits and wassailers, once upon a time when communities were small and television free; the old Russian villages had carol singers too, traveling from house to house with images of stars and a boat, to represent the winter sun sailing through the darkness of the underworld. Carols, circle dances, children's games, even Mummers' Plays centered on death and rebirth: they all echoed to and fro, and so they did in the many drafts of the Revels program that was gradually built that year.

Many months later, Americans and Russians came together. Here's part of a description I wrote at the time:

> Dmitri Pokrovsky is rehearsing the Revels chorus in a church hall, a dark-red sweater pulled over his shirt against the first chill of October. His right hand holds a sheaf of music, his left hand beats time; he is teaching American singers to make sounds they've never imagined before, in a language they can't understand. "Like this, like a <u>sheep</u>!" he says to a soprano, and drops on all fours, bleating.

Challenge overcomes hilarity: down on her knees, the bemused soprano finds herself producing perfectly the strange nasal vibrato of Slavic folk song. Then she stands up, opens her mouth to go on singing—and sounds instantly like an American. Dmitri grins, and points her to her knees again.

The rehearsal bounces along for hours, through energetic stamping dances taught step-by-step to our delighted, sweating American chorus by Pokrovsky and his associate, Tatyana "Tanya" Nekludova. Pokrovsky is in shirtsleeves now, his forehead glistening; he rolls his eyes, but gives a last spirited fast-footed demonstration. Then he is back with the music, teaching a tongue-twisting sequence of syllables that the chorus can learn only through blind phonetic faith. One singer wails that she will never get them right.

Dmitri gives her a big reassuring beam. "Listen! If you make mistake nobody will know, because they don't speak Russian. And me I will forgive you. And Tanya she will block ears."

He murmurs to Tatyana in Russian and obligingly she covers her ears. Dmitri begins leading the chorus again: "Pie-doo vwee-doo dah nah voo-lee-tsoo . . ."

Tatyana Nekludova led most of the subsequent Cambridge rehearsals of Russian material, but she spoke no English, so assistant producer Kate, our only Russian speaker, made the chorus a helpful list of phonetic translations under the heading "WHAT IS SHE *SAYING*?!" It went on to offer a range of phrases they might find handy in communicating with the ten chorus members of the Pokrovsky Ensemble, most of whom spoke no English either. For instance:

KAK DYELA' ? (How are things?)
   And in answer:
KHA-RA-SHO' (Good)
NAR-MA'L-NO' soft L (Not too bad, the usual)
NYE SPRASI' (Don't ask!)

The Pokrovsky Ensemble took off for Alaska in early November, to begin a concert tour that would end with the two Revels productions, first in California and then in Cambridge. While they were gone, Jack had some chest pain that even he couldn't ignore, and his cardiologist gave him a stress test whose result was so abnormal that it was reported as "strange that he didn't suffer pain during it." An angiogram showed "widespread arterial disease," and he went into the hospital for an angioplasty. I flew back that day from giving a lecture in Seattle and found a note on my desk saying, "Jack is fine after this morning's op — a bit groggy, but he says he'll be at rehearsal next week."

And so he was. His family and his close friends knew that every day of his presence thereafter was a bonus, but it was easy to forget because Jack himself, though taking his pills and paying due attention to diet and exercise, declined to give the matter any attention. He was far too involved with living to give any thought to death, which is probably a major reason why he lived on until 2005.

He didn't sing and dance "The Lord of the Dance" in the Russian-American Revels, however; Mark Baker and David Coffin alternated in performing it for him. Nor did he direct the show; it was produced by Revels veteran Lynne Beasley and directed on both coasts by Paddy Swanson.

Both in California and Cambridge, this Revels electrified its audiences, from the moment when a great blast of horns at the back of the theater heralded Dmitri and the other Russian men bounding down the aisles singing at the tops of their voices: "Cossack Epic Song," it was called, and it certainly was. A riotously bicultural show ended with breakneck Appalachian and Russian Mummers' Plays sharing the same death-and-rebirth theme, and the entire company dived together, more or less bilingually, into the traditional Revels "Sussex Mummers Carol."

After which, Sanders Theatre erupted into a roar of celebratory *glasnost* delight. It was a joyous show, and the collaboration was repeated later in the Houston Revels and on a CD — though Jack never achieved his ultimate goal of taking it to Moscow.

Six years later, Dmitri — less fortunate than his American twin — died in Moscow of heart failure. He was fifty-two years old.

Chapter Fourteen

"I've got so much more . . ."

*I*n his seventies Jack became a busy missionary, traveling from one Revels to another, advising communities who wanted a Revels, lecturing, teaching, and giving workshops on teaching music to children, at colleges and universities all over the United States — at home, notably at Simmons, Lesley, and Wheelock. Both he and Nancy were deeply involved in promoting the place of the arts in the classroom; after joining the faculty at Lesley, Nancy eventually founded and ran its Creative Arts in Learning master's program, with Jack as one of the artist-teachers. He still kept up his connection with the Pinewoods music camp; he still sang the occasional concert; he never stopped going.

This kind of routine was not popular with his cardiologist, but Jack's attitude toward his health had a lot in common with Queen Victoria's famous remark about the Boer War: *We are not interested in the possibilities of defeat; they do not exist.* Angioplasty had provided only temporary help for his diseased arteries, and by November 1993 he was in the hospital for a quadruple bypass operation. He spoke of it rather as if it had been a tiresome attack of the flu, and he had no compunction about appearing in a Mesoamerican Revels in California in 1998 stripped to the waist, with his railroad-track scar clearly visible on his chest.

But he became a little more careful after the bypass; his energy was no longer unlimited. David Coffin, who took over what he refers to as "the part that Jack built" onstage at Sanders Theatre, remembers Jack performing for the last time in Cambridge at the twenty-fifth-anniversary Revels in 1995:

He was doing the evening shows while I did the matinees — he was conserving his strength. "The Twelve Days of Christmas" was in that show, and it's long; the audience is divided into three parts and you have to direct them — it takes a lot of energy. One night I was standing there in the chorus, and just before the song I suddenly felt a firm hand on my back and Jack's voice in my ear: "David, you do it." And he propelled me to the front of the stage. No warning. And twelve hundred people looking at me expectantly.

So he did it, of course, for the man he — like so many — describes as his mentor.

I learned so much about being onstage just from standing behind him, the first ten years I did Revels in Cambridge. Today when I teach the audience the songs for the second half, I feel Jack's presence. And when I sing "The Lord of the Dance," it's his voice I still hear, not mine.

We all learned from him. Even as a writer, I learned from him. Sometime in the 1990s I mentioned to Jack that I was haunted by the idea of writing a book about a modern boy actor who finds himself transported back to play in Shakespeare's company at the old Globe Theatre. Then I wrote a different book instead.

A whole year later Jack said, "Are you going to write your Shakespeare book?"

"Oh . . . I don't know."

"I'd love to read it," he said.

But I was busy with a screenplay, on some wildly different subject.

A few months later he presented me with a copy of John Bennett's *Master Skylark,* a long out-of-print book that he had managed to hunt down in a secondhand bookshop. It's about an Elizabethan boy actor.

He said, "I thought it might encourage you to write about your boy."

I groaned. "I'd have to do so much research."

A few weeks later he rang up and said, "Are you writing your Shakespeare book yet?"

So before long I was deep in academic histories of sixteenth-century theater companies, and flying to London to examine the rebuilt Globe Theatre. When my book *King of Shadows* came out in 1999, I sent Jack the first copy. Inscribed, of course, "For Jack, without whom —"

It had been his persistence, not mine, that produced one of my best books, but he shrugged off any suggestion of responsibility. At the dinner celebrating Revels' twenty-fifth anniversary, he listened to people praising his accomplishment, with an expression of discomfort bordering on pain. The pattern hadn't changed since he was a choirboy: he loved the power his singing had over an audience, and enjoyed the applause, but once offstage he flinched from any exposure unrelated to his voice. It was almost as though his talent were an independent entity ("the Voice," he had called it, in those early letters home), and he its servant. Maybe he felt, in some cavern of the unconscious, that creating Revels was part of the service. As Paddy Swanson once put it, "Jack has no visible ego whatsoever."

Here's one other instance. In the early drafts of the script for the Victorian Revels in 1977, there was always a gap before the final "Sussex Mummers Carol." Jack had written simply, "Verse." This being an age before the arrival of Google, I spent months scouring every available anthology, and offered him verse by Robert Herrick, T. S. Eliot, Walter de le Mare, Longfellow, and William Morris, and that productive person Anon. He kept shaking his head regretfully. One poem by Eleanor Farjeon nearly made the cut, but in the end he shook his head again. "It's not Revels," he said.

So I wrote him one. It was called "The Shortest Day," and although its fifteenth line originally included a reference to the "Old Queen" for the Victorian Revels, this is the way it ended up:

So the shortest day came, and the year died,
And everywhere down the centuries of the snow-white world
Came people singing, dancing, to drive the dark away.
They lighted candles in the winter trees,
They hung their homes with evergreen,
They burned beseeching candles all night long
To keep the year alive.
And when the new year's sunshine blazed awake
They shouted, revelling.
Through all the frosty ages you can hear them
Echoing, behind us — listen!
All the long echoes sing the same delight

This shortest day,
As promise wakens in the sleeping land;
They carol, feast, give thanks,
And dearly love their friends, and hope for peace.
And so do we, here, now,
This year and every year.
Welcome Yule!

Jack liked it, which was a great relief.

I said, "And after you shout that last 'Welcome Yule!' maybe the chorus can shout it after you."

"Good idea," said Jack, but he was smiling that faintly evasive smile that always meant he was dodging something.

"You *are* going to do it yourself, aren't you?"

"Well . . . I don't know. . . ."

"Why not?"

"Well . . . I might forget the words."

"You've been learning words all your life, for Pete's sake!"

"That was for singing," Jack said, still evasive.

"Jack, I *wrote* it for *you.*"

But even emotional blackmail didn't work. The chorus did indeed shout, "Welcome Yule!" and so, instinctively, did most of the audience, but the poem was recited by Robert J. Lurtsema. He did it very nicely, but it wasn't what I had heard in my head. To get Jack to stand up onstage at that particularly theatrical moment, I should have written a song.

Almost two decades later, in 2003, Jack sent me a postcard from Greece, where he was on vacation with his family. It was a long time since we had collaborated on a Revels, and I was living in Connecticut, married by then to Hume Cronyn. Jack's postcard was a picture of the amazing amphitheater at Epidaurus, where, they say, even a whisper from the center of the stage can be heard anywhere in that great hemisphere.

"Susan dear," Jack wrote, "I knew Hume had once stood here and done a speech, so I thought of you both yesterday as I stood at the center spot and recited 'The Shortest Day.'"

The poem is still a part of every Christmas Revels, and I do have a tape of Jack reciting it for a radio program, but I wish I'd been there that day at Epidaurus.

Until Revels' twenty-fifth anniversary, Jack, Paddy Swanson, and George Emlen were a happy artistic triumvirate, with Gayle Rich as Executive Director of the whole still-growing enterprise and long-time Revels mainstays like Alan Casso and Sue Ladr heading a staff of eight. Paddy was directing all the shows in Cambridge and some elsewhere. Jack made frequent western trips, as Revels acquired its eighth city in 1993, with the Puget Sound Revels, in Tacoma, Washington, and its ninth in 1995, in Portland, Oregon. In 1995 he handed over artistic leadership to Paddy, became Director Emeritus and "retired"—but went on giving Revels performances in California, Minnesota, and Illinois, and working on the educational outreach programs that are today as important a part of Revels, Inc., as its solstice celebrations.

One of these was the Langstaff Teaching Video Project. To finance it, Lisby Mayer, the remarkable psychoanalyst who was also founder and director of the California Revels, had in 1992 already begun the hefty task of raising $87,000. Filmed in California, this enterprise eventually produced two sets of two videocassettes in 1995, *Making Music in the Classroom* and—for use at home—*Making Music with Children.* They show just that: Jack teaching children to make music. Quite apart from their practical value for parents and teachers, they are probably a better record of the man who made the Revels than any documentation of the things he actually said *about* the Revels.

He had two groups of children, about fifteen in each: one group aged four to seven, the other seven to ten. We see him teaching them, every morning for two weeks, interspersed with his commentary on what's happening, and gradually we see them learning, more by a kind of osmosis than by overt instruction. Jack gets down on the floor with them but he doesn't talk down to them; he just talks, sings, shows them what to do, and does it with them. He says in voice-over commentary, at one point: "Everyone's got this — let's bring it out of them." It is all very much the way he used to rehearse the Revels chorus children, in the early years: there was always an implicit assumption of success, as if he were not teaching a land animal how to swim, but teaching a fish how to swim better.

George Emlen says today: "It was unusual to teach songs the way Jack did. The way he sits on the floor with them in the videos — most people would be at the piano, talking to them over their shoulder. He had that sense of spontaneity, having fun yet always able to quell a disturbance by going past it. There was always joy bubbling up."

A small child says, in the film, beaming, "When I feel like singing, I just can't hold it in, I have to *sing.*"

Jack teaches them the traditional songs and singing games that he had recorded and used in the Revels, and on BBC radio and television decades earlier: "Sally Go Round the Moon," "Over in the Meadow," "Cocky Robin" . . .

Who killed Cocky Robin?
Who killed Cocky Robin?
I, said the Sparrow,

185

With my little bow and arrow,
It was I, it was I.

Who saw him die?
Who saw him die?
I, said the Fly,
With my little teensy eye,
It was I, it was I.

Who caught his blood?
Who caught his blood?
I, said the Fish,
With my little silver dish,
It was I, it was I. . . .

The children love it, and when he asks them if the song is sad or happy, unanimously they choose the second. It's all about death, and in considerable vivid detail, but as he points out in commentary: "They say it's a happy song — because of its sassy little tune." The music has more power than the words. And he keeps the children moving, and makes them listen to the notes they are singing. "All song should have the quality of dance," he says.

In the video of the older group in particular, you can see a telling progression in the children's ease with rhythm and the patterns of music. There are small bemused faces at the start, when he goes around the circle making each of them find a rhythm in the words of his or her own name, but before long they are moving and chanting to "Mango Walk" ("*Spit* out the words!"), coping with a mix of simultaneous street cries, singing a little two-part canon. By the end he even has them taking part in the collaborative pattern of a very basic orchestra.

He says, "Working with children, with music, you are working with magic, really."

In 2004, Jack performed in Britten's *Noye's Fludde* for the last time. Over the years he had played Noye often; this time, he was the Voice of God in a Revels production directed by Paddy Swanson and conducted by George Emlen—at the same First Church in Cambridge where Revels had first had its offices. God is the only speaking part in *Noye's Fludde,* and Britten specified that "he should ideally be placed high up and away from the stage." So Jack was in the balcony; you can hear his voice ringing out, obeying Britten's stage direction *"tremendous,"* in a video posted on YouTube by Sue Ladr of Revels. He observed to George afterward that it was extremely strange to be looking down on the Ark after all these years, instead of looking up at God.

George, who gets to lead thousands in song at the Revels' annual RiverSing, an outdoor celebration of the autumn equinox, is one of those who consider Jack their mentor.

He had that quiet but powerful energy—he taught me how to engage and hold a crowd of any size with simple gestures, sincere intention, and utter conviction. He had incredibly high musical standards, and he was passionate about his art. And there was nothing ordinary about anything he did or thought—every day was an adventure. Anything could be "quite wonderful"—a performance, a meal, a drink, a poem. He'd say excitedly, almost conspiratorially, "I've got some Meyer lemons—they're the best. Come on, I'll make you a martini with Meyer lemons; they're incredible."

In his later years he would slip into the office and visit us one by one, catching up and making his apologetic but insistent requests. "Can you really make CDs from these old tapes?

*That's really incredible. Whenever you have time," he'd say,
handing me a plastic bag full of old cassettes. "Just anytime.
No hurry." And before long he'd have slipped out again. . . .*
  *Above all, if there's one word for what Jack always did, it
is empowerment. He treated each of us as a collaborator. And
he was so effective with audiences because he had this conviction that everyone not only could sing but wanted to sing, and
even needed to sing, even if they didn't know it. So of course
they did.*

Then there was CLNE, which is as good a symbol as any for
his lifetime involvement with all kinds of education. Almost every
year from 1986 until the year he died, Jack and I spent a week each
summer at a peripatetic one-week conference known as Children's
Literature New England. For two decades this remarkable institution was, in the small world of children's books, a high point of the
year: a demanding sequence of lectures and workshops with celebrated speakers; a recharging of professional batteries; an affectionate family gathering. It would culminate in the unlikely sight of
some two hundred teachers and librarians, writers and artists, outdoors on some university campus holding hands in a gigantic circle
and singing "Wild Mountain Thyme," alongside the soaring baritone of John Langstaff.

Jack had been part of it from the beginning. In 1975 a remarkable teacher named Barbara Harrison, believing passionately that
children's books should be treated not as teaching tools but as literature, won a grant from the National Endowment for the Humanities
to found and direct the Center for the Study of Children's Literature at Simmons College, in Boston. She was driven by the same
inspired obstinacy with which Jack was simultaneously setting up
the Christmas Revels. Indeed, Jack was one of the participants in

a 1975 summer institute that Barbara organized, at Simmons's request, to "prove the marketability of a children's literature program." The participants in his seminar were there to "explore ways of involving children in folk literature and music." The novelist Gregory Maguire, who attended it, was at twenty-two the Center's first and most notable graduate student—and briefly, in a nice familial connection, a member of the Revels chorus. (Eventually he became deputy director of the Center, and later wrote a book called *Wicked*, which was turned, as you may have noticed, into a musical.)

The Center flourished from 1977 onward, with a rich array of graduate courses, a broad outreach program, and a regular one-week summer institute that became famous for its literary focus. From the beginning, Jack was part of it, generally giving a talk about the ballads. Then in 1986, the sky fell in: Simmons decided that the Center, hitherto autonomous, should become part of the Department of Education. It was a small decision with stupendous implications, since it would negate the Center's whole original *raison d'être* as a focus on children's books as literature rather than primarily a tool for teaching.

Barbara, Greg, and their founding faculty members protested bitterly, and eventually resigned. And out of this academic explosion CLNE was born: an independent, floating conference that dropped anchor for a week every August on a university campus, somewhere in the eastern United States, England, or Ireland. It was a demanding, uncompromising celebration of excellence in children's books as literature, approached every year from a different angle, as some sample themes show: *Swords and Ploughshares; Worlds Apart; Rogues and Rebels; The Heroic Ideal* . . .

There we all happily were, every first week in August, talking about books: writers, illustrators, librarians, teachers, and the

189

students who would receive four continuing education units as academic credit for their hardworking week. Every morning's core lecture was based on a reading list, and every evening lecture drew on the whole corpus of children's literature. Both Jack and I generally did talks, but besides that he was essential to the basic fabric and mood of the week. He made them all sing. At the start of the week and again every morning, he would bound up to the stage, usually in white shirt and pants, a Morris man without the bells, and lead them in folk song or canon, familiar or strange. It put music into their minds, the rhythm and harmony they would be finding in prose and verse for the rest of their time there — and it illuminated every day.

He trained them to sing grace before dinner, too, using the same easy skill with which he trained Revels audiences to sing carols. I've never forgotten the first night's dinner at a CLNE institute at Newnham College, Cambridge — the English Cambridge, the original one — when Jack stood up and raised one arm, and the entire dining hall erupted into four-part harmony with *Praise . . . God . . . For . . . Meat.* The college servants who were running around serving us all stopped in their tracks, astounded, and one of them dropped a plate.

The driving perfectionism of CLNE kept argument and celebration humming through each of these weeks, even outside the punishing schedule of lectures: over coffee in Harvard Square or walks through the Backs, depending on which Cambridge we were in; in college gardens, in dormitory bathrooms, or (more loudly) over communal bottles of wine in dorm rooms at the end of the day. A passion for good books is infectious. And at intervals Jack and I would sit in quiet corners discussing the next Christmas program for Revels.

The penultimate CLNE was held in 2005 at Radcliffe University, four months before Jack died; he led that intent summer audience in the folk songs whose words hold the roots of so many children's books, just as he had the first time thirty years earlier. I was staying with him in Cambridge, driving him to and fro. Though he chose not to think about it, his arteries were now in a truly perilous state, and Nancy had made sure I had the telephone numbers of his doctors in my pocket. As we were leaving the house the first morning, Jack paused in his garden and picked a red rose.

"What's that for?" I said.

"You'll see," said Jack.

And so I did, because the rose was in a glass of water onstage when he began the institute with music, and he had everyone singing "Fair Rosa," the Sleeping Beauty story, jaunty and poignant as all folk song. The rose stayed on that stage all through the week; each day it dropped a petal or two, but it glowed there till the end, when Jack's voice sent the CLNE audience reluctantly off to the outside world, trying like Fair Rosa to take the magic with them.

Fair Rosa now will sleep no more
Sleep no more
Sleep no more
Fair Rosa now will sleep no more
A long time ago. . . .

As I said at the beginning, this book is not a biography of John Langstaff, nor a history of the Revels; it's a portrait of a Maker, subjective and incomplete. Perhaps it's a posthumous present to a friend. If Jack had written his book *The Choirboy*, there's no knowing whether he would have taken it past the beginning of Revels, Inc.; his initial impulse was simply to show how the roots of the Revels went way back into his childhood. He didn't want to document every aspect of his career, just as he didn't want to spread every detail of his private life out for public view.

So I haven't done those things either. This has just been a sketch, by someone who was once the tame Revels writer, of the man I knew and worked with. Dozens of people could produce one of their own, and they would all be different — and complementary. They would each certainly have a different focus: his singing, his recordings, his later outreach work with all the Revels cities; his teaching, and his work with Nancy on the importance of the arts in education; his place in the world of folk song and dance, and on and on.

Jack loved music, but above all he loved people; he was an enthusiast, a life enhancer, one of those people who light up the world. Though he avoided belonging to any specific church or even religion, and took care that Revels should do the same, he was a deeply spiritual man; at heart, he was still the choirboy who felt he was singing to God. I think he'd have liked the fact that the crew of the space shuttle *Discovery* were awakened one morning in 2007 by — at the request of its commander's husband — the voice of John Langstaff singing "The Lord of the Dance." It's the ultimate celebration, perhaps, to have your voice traveling out into space, out into the mystery, paying tribute, spreading joy.

His professional relationships nearly always became friendships, and lasted. He loved best his still center: Tro, as he always called Nancy; his children; his siblings; the cabin in Vermont, and a few other tranquil places where he could listen to the silence. But his mind and imagination whirled with energy, all his life. The last time I spent the night with him and Nancy in the Cambridge house, eleven days before he died, his face fell when he found I had to leave next morning. "I've got so much more for us to talk about," he said. "All sorts of ideas . . ."

A few days later he flew to Switzerland to visit his daughter

Deborah, her minister husband, Burkhard, and their two small daughters. The girls found him sitting in a chair one morning, looking, they said, surprised. He had had a major stroke. He lived long enough for Nancy to fly from Boston to join him, and to feel him squeeze her hand, and then he died peacefully with his family singing to him. When Burkhard presided at the memorial for John Meredith Langstaff months later, at Harvard Memorial Church, in Cambridge, he followed a program precisely designed by its subject. Jack's knowledge of his own fragility had given him the chance to choose for a last time the words, the music, the cast — and most characteristic of all, to stress, said Burkhard, that this should be not a matter for grief but "a celebration of life and an expression of gratitude."

His ashes lie at the center of a stone labyrinth that was one of his last eager projects; he and the family set it out on the hillside near the Vermont house. Though it's there for meditation, it employs of course the same ancient circling pattern around which Jack led his joyful Revels audiences every year as the Lord of the Dance. The labyrinth was finished not too long before he died; he was very pleased with it. The wind sings through the trees, up there, under a quiet sky. By the time of the winter solstice, the hillside is deep in snow.

But the seasons turn, in their own time, and before long, sweet spring is out. The scent of the lilacs drifts over the labyrinth. You can almost hear that voice, full of delight and gaiety and tumultuous, irrepressible ideas.

—⁓◎ Books by John Langstaff ◎⁓—

A Revels Garland of Song

The Christmas Revels Songbook, with Nancy Langstaff

Climbing Jacob's Ladder: Heroes of the Bible in African-American Spirituals, illustrated by Ashley Bryan

Frog Went A-Courtin', illustrated by Feodor Rojankovsky

The Golden Vanity, illustrated by David Gentleman

Hi! Ho! The Rattlin' Bog and Other Folk Songs for Group Singing, illustrated by Robin Jacques

Hot Cross Buns and Other Old Street Cries, illustrated by Nancy Winslow Parker

"I Have A Song to Sing, O!" An Introduction to the Songs of Gilbert and Sullivan, illustrated by Emma Chichester Clark

Jim Along, Josie: A Collection of Folk Songs and Singing Games for Young Children, with Nancy Langstaff, illustrated by Jan Pieńkowski

Making Music: How to Create and Play Seventy Homemade Musical Instruments, with Ann Sayre Wiseman

Oh, A-Hunting We Will Go, illustrated by Nancy Winslow Parker

Ol' Dan Tucker, illustrated by Joe Krush

On Christmas Day in the Morning: A Traditional Carol, illustrated by Melissa Sweet

Over in the Meadow, illustrated by Feodor Rojankovsky

Revels Book of Chanteys and Sea Songs, with George Emlen

Saint George and the Dragon: A Mummer's Play,
with David Gentleman

*Sally Go Round the Moon: Revels Songs and Singing Games for
Young Children*, with Nancy Langstaff, illustrated by Jan Pieńkowski

*Shimmy Shimmy Coke-Ca-Pop! A Collection of City Children's
Street Games and Rhymes*, with Carol Langstaff, photographs by
Don MacSorley

Soldier, Soldier, Won't You Marry Me?, illustrated by Anita Lobel

The Swapping Boy, illustrated by Beth and Joe Krush

*Sweetly Sings the Donkey: Animal Rounds for Children to Sing or
Play on Recorders*, illustrated by Nancy Winslow Parker

The Two Magicians, illustrated by Fritz Eichenberg

What a Morning! The Christmas Story in Black Spirituals,
illustrated by Ashley Bryan

───∾◎ Recordings by John Langstaff ◎∾───

These have all been reissued on CD by Revels, Inc.

At the Foot of Yonder Mountain
(Appalachian ballads and folksongs, with John Powell at the
piano, 1961)

The Lark in the Morn
(folk songs and ballads recorded at Abbey Road 1949–1956)

Nottamun Town
(British and American folk songs and ballads, accompanied on
guitar by Martin Best, recorded for EMI in 1964)

Songs for Singing Children
*John Langstaff Sings The Jackfish and More Songs for Singing
Children*
(both the above recorded in the 1950s and 1960s at Abbey Road
Studios in Britain, produced by George Martin)

The Water Is Wide
(American and British folksongs and ballads, originally released
by Tradition Records in 1959)

—◦❧ Revels Today ❧◦—

The heart of Revels is still in Massachusetts. With Patrick Swanson as Artistic Director and Steve Smith as Executive Director, Revels Inc. has passed its 40th birthday. The national office is at 80 Mount Auburn Street, Watertown, Massachusetts 02472, and though Christmas Revels performances at Harvard's Sanders Theatre are still the peak of the year for the parent company, a whole calendar of its other activities can be found at Revels.org

The website will also lead you to details of the nine other production companies in the Revels family:

California Revels	Artistic Director, David Parr
	Executive Director, Dirk Burns
Revels Houston	Artistic Director, Beth Sanford
	Executive Director, Peggy Curtis
New York Revels	Producer, Nancy Petaja
Revels North	Artistic Director, Maureen Burford
	Producer, Sherry Merrick
Portland Revels	Executive Director, Debby Garman
Puget Sound Revels	Executive Director, Mary Lynn

Rocky Mountain Revels   Producer, Karen Romeo

Santa Barbara Revels   Producer, Susan Keller

Washington Revels   Artistic Director, Roberta Gasbarre
Executive Director, Greg Lewis